Law Business School

The MBA for Your Law Practice

ALEXANDRA LOZANO, ESQ.

ALLY LOZANO LLC

For permissions, email **info@allylozano.com**

ISBN 978-1-7320825-2-6

Ally Lozano, LLC

16400 Southcenter Parkway Suite 306

Tukwila, WA 98188

www.AllyLozano.com

Disclaimer

This book is presented solely for educational and entertainment purposes. This is not legal advice and should not be construed as such. Furthermore, an attorney must always comply with his or her bar rules and regulations. The author and publisher are not offering this book as legal, accounting, or other professional services advice. While best efforts have been used in preparing this book, the author and publisher make no representations or warranties of any kind and assume no liability of any kind with respect to the accuracy or completeness of the contents. Neither the author nor the publisher shall be held liable or responsible to any person or entity with respect to any loss or incidental or consequential damages caused, or alleged to have been caused, directly or indirectly, by the information contained herein. Every company is different and the advice and strategies contained herein may not be suitable for your situation.

Dedication

To Amy Rios, my right-hand, my confidant, and my friend. You have been a part of every success. Finding you has been one of the greatest gifts of my life. Thank you for everything.

Foreword

As the owner of a successful law firm, I often look back and wish that I had gotten a degree in business before pursuing my law degree. Law school prepares us to fight for justice and advocate for our clients, but it does not prepare us to run a business.

Many attorneys open their own practice believing that they will just figure it out - that the clients will come, the bills will get paid, the work will get done - only to find themselves drowning months later. Potential clients aren't calling. Existing clients aren't paying. Case files are disorganized, and staff is neglecting their work.

Without the knowledge necessary to run a business, all the responsibilities pile up until the attorney doesn't even enjoy the law anymore. What was once an exciting venture becomes the anxiety that keeps the attorney up at night, and she wonders if she should just close the firm.

Are you having similar thoughts about your law firm? Or maybe you're considering opening your own practice, but these worries are preventing you from taking the leap. Either way, you're not alone. These are the struggles that hundreds of attorneys face as business owners, and up until now, we just had to deal with it and figure it out alone. But not anymore.

That's where Ally comes in. Ally built a thriving law practice from scratch, and she continues to build her business each day. She has found innovative solutions to make running a law firm seem easy. Her systems allow attorneys to enjoy practicing the law and make a lot of money doing it.

In this book, Ally gives a step-by-step guide to running, and thriving in, your law practice. She takes everything you should have learned in a law school business management class (if such a thing existed), and distills it into a comprehensive, easy-to-read, inspirational guide.

Ally teaches you about finances and shows you how to get paid for the amazing work you do. She trains you on marketing your firm and attracting the right clients. She explains how to manage staff and create effective processes to streamline your workflow. Everything you need to know about running a law firm is in this book, and it's easy to understand and implement.

Since opening my practice in 2014, I have experienced ups and downs. I've faced financial struggles. I've hired and fired employees. I've tried out different systems and software. I've figured out, after lots of experimentation, how to effectively communicate with clients and keep them happy. I've done a lot, and it wasn't always easy.

Looking back, I wish this book had been available when I started my practice. Implementing the guidance Ally provides in this book from the beginning would have allowed me to build my firm on a solid foundation. I wouldn't have had to second-guess. I would have saved hours of research and trial-and-error. And I would have made a lot more money a lot sooner in my practice.

This is the book every law firm owner needs to read (and dog-ear, and highlight, and read again). It is a true guide to running a law firm like a business owner, making money, and loving every second of it!

- Lauren A. Eagan, Esq.
Owner and Founder of Eagan Immigration PLLC
CEO of Corner Office Queen

Contents

Introduction

I wrote this book, The *Law Firm Business School*, because law school didn't teach us to be business people. They taught us to be lawyers and then threw us out into the world with our licenses to run a "solo practice"- never using the word "business." That's why so many lawyers don't even consider our solo and small firms a business. But a law firm is a business and if we don't figure out how to run a business, our law firms will fail. By fail, I don't necessarily mean that your doors will close, rather that you will run yourself into the ground. You will not ever get a break, even on vacation (or maybe you feel like you can't take a vacation). You will constantly feel overwhelmed. You will be stuck in the cycle of charging too little and working too much. Maybe you are already there and want a change but you don't know how to make it.

It's time to run your law firm like a business. It's scary because you probably don't know how to run a business. I surely didn't. But I learned and figured it out and created a 7-figure law firm as a solo practitioner. Here's the good news- I've made a ton of mistakes and done the hard work of figuring out how to run a law firm like the business that it is, that way you can skip all of the mistakes and jump directly to having success in your law practice.

Here I compile the business lessons I learned and discovered, as well as the techniques I myself had to invent out of necessity.

When I first went solo, I continued operating the way we've been trained to operate. I used the same procedures you usually find in most law firms. It took some hard knocks to make me realize I needed to change how we do things if I wanted to change how I earned and live a life that I absolutely love.

I hope this book arms you with everything you need to run your firm as a business. That means controlling your finances, managing your staff without getting stuck in the middle of them, treating your clients as the heartbeat of your law firm, and more.

Business isn't scary, it's fun! I will show you the way.

I know that success beyond your wildest dreams is standing right in front of you, so let's go get it.

Chapter 1: Mindset

We all have a set of beliefs. We have picked them up over our lifetime and now they are ingrained in our psyche. We don't even notice them, but they can and do stop us from success.

Beliefs about being content with "enough" money, excuses we tell ourselves on why we're not becoming successful, excesses in things of no use to our business and our wellness, putting ourselves down, wearing ourselves to the bone due to perfectionism, and underearning even when clients *can* pay us...

Do those sound familiar? A lot of this has to do with our upbringing and our peers—stories we were told as children that only persisted into adulthood. It's what we see our peers doing, so it's just what we do as well. We accept the status quo and we don't challenge it. We become prisoners to our limiting beliefs.

Many of these beliefs are completely wrong. To start making more money and becoming the CEO of your law firm, you need to discover *and* fix all the kinks in your mindset that hold you back from treating your law firm as a real business.

Money Mindset and Overcoming Excuses

In order to begin to make more money, we have to look at our money mindset and the excuses we tell ourselves about why we're not successful. If we are underearning, or if we are earning well but not earning at our highest potential, it likely has to do with our way of thinking and our excuses.

The treacherous part of excuses is that they are usually based on truths about ourselves and our present circumstances. It can be dangerously easy to justify why things aren't working out the way that you want or need them to.

We all have reasons and excuses for:

- not having the success that we want

- not having the lives that we want

- not having the partner we want

- not having the clients we want

We have money stories: incorrect beliefs about money

A lot of financial stress has to do with our upbringing and stories that we were told since we were children.

For example, I was taught that the middle class way was the "best" way—even though my parents didn't use those words to describe it. You work hard. You get paid a good enough salary. You save up for your retirement through work, maybe put a little money in the stock market. And then you retire, and *that's* when you get to enjoy your life.

Another incorrect belief: If something was a "good deal" then I should buy it. I could need it one day!

These beliefs were completely wrong and led to me overspending, underearning, being stuck in jobs that I didn't like just because of "the benefits" and more. What are some of your money stories?

We feel bad charging our clients

For years I was stuck earning $20–$30k a year. Part of the reason I couldn't earn more was that when it came down to charging my clients, I felt bad. I felt like they earned less money and had less education than me. And I thought, "Poor them, I would be 'taking' money from them."

Even when I *knew* that they were earning more money than me, I still justified under earning and undercharging with, "Well I have more than I could ever want and need, and they need the money more than I do."

YES, I seriously thought this! In the face of them owning more, earning more, and having more than me! It shows how out of whack my thinking was.

How to fix your money mindset and overcome your excuses

Step 1: Recognize the incorrect money stories you are telling yourself.

Here are the most common money stories that I've heard from lawyers:

- It's greedy to earn money.

- My partner or spouse has a good job, so I don't really need to earn a lot of money.

- My clients aren't as well off as I am, so I shouldn't charge them.

- I don't care about money. I don't want to have money.

- I have everything I need, so why should I want more?

- I'm comfortable. That's all I want is to be comfortable.

- I'll enjoy life when I retire. Right now I need to work.

- I can't ask for a raise right now because my boss says there's no more money.

- If I ask for a raise, I'll just be told no.

- I don't need to buy anything fancy. I don't mind shopping for discounts.

- I love deals. Why would I pay full price when I can get it on sale?

Here are the most common excuses we tell ourselves:

- *"I tried to start a firm before, and I failed, so why wouldn't I fail again?"*

- *"I am going to disappoint my family, because I am not good enough to do this."*

- *"If I only had _____ (i.e. money, looks, education, etc.), it would be happening for me. But since I don't have that, it isn't."*

Do those thoughts sound like yours? Hear them out without judgment. Just recognize them. Pay extra attention to them.

Step 2: Change the story and listen to what's true.

Just as you have money stories, which are false and/or limiting, you have money truths, which are real and true to your personality, desires, and goals.

It may be that you truly love a good bargain. In your firm, this translates to maximizing your time and staff roles.

I judged myself a lot for my personal truth that I want to be "rich." I thought that meant that I was greedy, stuck up, mean, selfish, and more. I realized that I had to challenge myself to take away the stigma and the incorrect beliefs that I had around wealth and aiming for financial success.

It's the same for excuses. Change the story. Reframe it: *"I tried to run a law firm before, and it didn't work out. But I am different now and it will work out for me this time."*

Don't let your incorrect belief systems and excuses control you and hinder you. Decide your truths. You can say, "Okay, that may be true, but I'm going to try it anyway." **Or let go of the old truth all together!** Anything that holds you back doesn't serve you. You can decide to just let it go.

Step 3: Reprogram the incorrect beliefs. Challenge your excuses.

We need to cultivate a mindset to be stronger than our excuses and always talk back to what we believe. It is *easy* to fall pray to our excuses and old beliefs. It is harder to fight against them, change the way that we think, and keep charging forward.

"Talk back" to your beliefs. You know how pre-teens and teens have a response for *everything*—they always challenge what you say. If the sky is blue, then "Uh uh it's purple."

I want you to be like a preteen and give yourself a lot of back-talk as a gentle self-correction:

Your mind: I can't afford to go to Europe.
Your back talk: Of course I can go to Europe if I plan for it.

It's easy to stay stuck in old stories that justify reasons we can't do or have the things we want and need. Challenge them.

Step 4: Embrace your money truths and be hyper-aware of excuses.

Begin to shine huge floodlights on your excuses and old beliefs. Bring them out of the dark and into the light. Once you do, they don't feel so scary. (And you might also begin to see holes in them.)

It has been scientifically proven that people cling to things that make them miserable just because those things are familiar. People are so afraid of change that they prefer their old beliefs and excuses rather than go after what they want. It can be scary, can't it?

This is why it is difficult to embrace an entirely new way of thinking.

Allow yourself to feel uncomfortable. Sit with the judgment and the pain. Acknowledge it. release it.

My money truths were:

- I wanted to make more money.

- I wanted a lifestyle where I could travel a ton and do the work I love.

- I wanted to have a Range Rover, and more.

My mind was telling me I was going to fail. I better stay where I was because it was stable and I knew I could count on it. Why would I want anything more? Who was I to dare to ask for anything more?

I had to work through that negative self-talk. I knew my beliefs weren't true. My money truths were my goals and I embraced them.

My excuses were just that-- excuses. Whenever I find myself making an excuse, I dive right into it: What am I scared of? What am I telling myself? Why am I thinking this way? What can I do to change the way I see this?

Step 5: Release and Relief

When you work through these issues, you release them and you feel relief. You are free. The more you keep working on these issues, the more you release them instead of clinging to them. You get freer and freer to move forward to your goals.

Step 6: Speak your desires as truth.

This can be weird at first, but it works. "I am a millionaire." "I am a financially successful lawyer."

When you speak your desires or goals as if they've already happened, you cancel out old beliefs and any excuses that might try to contradict you. This is how you make it happen. You simply have something better in your head and you no longer hear your old beliefs and excuses.

Step 7: Always try on ideas first.

Excuses and your old mindset are never more persistent as when you face something new.

So try on ideas first. When you receive advice about something from a reliable source, instead of explaining all the ways that it won't work for you, try to find a way to make it work. You don't need to take every piece of advice that comes your way, but you want to make sure you give it a chance. You must be vigilant to ensure that you're not reflexively clinging to excuses that hold you back instead of trying new ways to propel yourself forward.

Your money mindset affirmation

I want you to overcome your excuses and have this money mindset breakthrough.

Once you begin to work through this, you will have a life and a business that's better than your wildest dreams. Deciding to turn your law firm into a successful business can be overwhelming. Fixing your money mindset and letting go of your tendency to cling to excuses are the first steps.

Here is your money mindset mantra:

I do great work. I deserve to make a great living.

I do excellent work. I deserve to make an excellent living.

I do the work I love. I have the life of my dreams.

Mantra for overcoming excuses:

It is going to be hard, but I am going to try it anyway.

I am successful in every way. I have the life of my dreams.

I am a businesswoman. I am a powerful CEO.

Believe in yourself. I know from experience that it's not an easy thing to do but you can do hard things. (Come on- you passed the bar!)

Next, you can give yourself peace of mind and address the overwhelm a great deal by embracing minimalism.

Embracing Minimalism

Minimalism can change your life. And the idea is simple—live with less. However you define "less" is up to you. The concept is you just stop overdoing, overspending, over-having, over- everything and just … enjoy. Live. Breathe. Be.

Badge of honor or bringer of doom?

I see overachiever behavior in so many lawyers. Lawyers talk about stress and over-extension as if it's a badge of honor.

But the problem is that all of this over-doing brings a whole slew of problems:

- Drama

- Negativity

- Cluttered mind

- Overwhelm

- Burnout

- Strained finances

Keeping up—or trying your hardest to.

We burn ourselves out, and while we're burning, we believe that our actions are exemplary because... "Look how much pro bono work I did!" "And look how little I charged for a case that you charged so much for!" "And look how many more hours I worked this week than everyone else."

Do those sound familiar?

It would be hard to find a lawyer who doesn't describe herself as overwhelmed. I think many lawyers have strained finances. And on top of that, our minds are cluttered with all of the tasks and the shoulds that we think are required to be lawyers.

Pushing the reset button.

Finally, I hit my breaking point. I was tired of the "too much" of my life. Working too much, drinking too much, obsessing too much, consuming too much, and more. I gave away half of what I owned, maybe more. I moved to Mexico and got rid of half of that.

From there I slowly started to get rid of more and more. And then a hurricane hit, and I lost everything that I owned. I was effectively forced into minimalism. That was the reset button I needed.

Now I focus on the things that I want out of my life. I make time for every single thing I want to do. I had to eliminate a lot of "extras" in order to get it there, but I can tell you that I wake up every day madly in love with my life.

Here are some of the major changes I made:

- I almost never watch TV.

    - My DVR used to be full, and I was always trying to "catch up" with shows I didn't really care about anyway.

- I have no drama in my life in any way at all. Even when there are difficult people in my life, there is still no drama—I just don't let it in.

    - I used to believe that drama would "find me everywhere" and that I truly was "no drama." I was the drama. And I brought it with me everywhere. It was exhausting and draining.

- I don't volunteer for organizations. Instead, I host my own free legal clinics. I host a FB live show where people can ask me legal questions for free. I organize my own fundraisers and drives for people in need in the communities to which I belong. By doing this, I make volunteerism work with my time and my schedule instead of bending over backwards to try to accommodate everything.

- I only buy things that I love, and get rid of things the second I can't use them or don't want them anymore.

- I used to have 20 coffee cups, a salad spinner, 5 spatulas, at least 30 cookbooks... and that's just the tip of the iceberg! Now I have the bare minimum.

- I am involved with my kids in the ways that I want to be. I don't do things because I feel like I "should" do them, nor do I judge other parents for their ways. I exist in my way and honor the ways of others.

- I handle everything the second that I start it. For example, I don't check the mail unless I am committed to dealing with it right at that moment. I don't begin a project that I cannot complete—even if it's a project I would love to do. I know that I won't pick it up later. I put things away immediately, and I don't keep them out for later.

- My house is spotless all of the time. I maintain it this way by having no clutter and not saving things for later.

  - My house always used to be a mess, filled with clutter, half-completed projects, and paperwork that I was "going to get to eventually."

- My car is clean all of the time.

  - My car was always a disaster. Always.

- I read constantly and voraciously. I love every second of it.

- I have time and make time for things that I love. Like AMIGA, writing and creating courses for AllyLozano.com. I write books. I write blogs. I spend time on social media. (And of course this is in addition to running my law firm, maintaining my marriage, and raising 5 kids.)

- My money is managed. It is invested. It is working for me at all times.

- I spend money on experiences instead of things. My kids have under 15 toys each.

- I travel monthly.

- I hardly ever drink alcohol at all.

- I stopped swearing.

Hopefully you won't have change forced on you as drastically as it had been for me with a near-breakdown and then a hurricane, but I do want to challenge you to deeply consider minimalism in your life. I know how incredible it feels to have a clear mind, a peaceful life and a clean home—things I never thought I would have before.

How to do–or start– the minimalist purge

You can start small. Then I challenge you to go bigger. The places where you can really get minimalist are:

- Your kitchen

- Your closet

- Your kids' toys

- Your office

Take the rooms one by one and do it until it's done. Get rid of anything that hasn't been used in 30 days. Don't save things "in case" you need them. When that day comes, you can go get them. For the meantime, give yourself the gift of your best life today- which means more mental space because you have less to weigh down your mind and your life.

Be ruthless.

Give yourself a set amount of time to FINISH—not to see how far you get, but to get it done. For example, give yourself 2 hours to go through your bedroom. Set a timer and get down to it.

If you force yourself to do it quickly, you will get rid of more because you won't overthink your decisions.

You do not need even a quarter of what you have.

In the kitchen, go for the minimum cups, glasses and plates. Caterers have plates and glasses. You don't need to be prepared for a dinner party.

In your linen closet, you don't need six sets of sheets. Get rid of four sets. Keep two. If any sheets or towels have holes in them, get rid of them.

Drop things off, or throw them away

This is part of the commitment to get rid of things: **if you carry them in your car then you carry them in your mind**. **So get on with getting rid of stuff right away**.

The next day, even if it's a workday, leave your house 15 minutes early to do a drop-off. That's it. Don't overcomplicate it or make it difficult, just do it.

Also, THROW THINGS AWAY.

I went to a lawyer's office to work with her one-on-one. We found papers in there from 1998! We hired a private trash pick up company to come all the office junk.

When it was done, she said she felt like she could breathe in her office for the first time. Her husband came in and was floored. He couldn't believe the place. He said it was incredible. We had thrown away all of the broken shelves and rearranged the nice furniture that she had in there. It looked like a brand new office.

It will transform you

We get used to the stuff lying around. We don't need them, we're just used to them, like a hole in a shirt or a faded dress.

When you commit to "a little less" of everything and clean out all excess—even just in one room, I guarantee you will instantly feel a sense of relief. It will transform you.

Each time you feel the urge to buy things, let it pass. Don't give in. Letting go of the need to consume is so freeing. With time, you will become addicted to giving things away and getting rid of things.

The purge can also mean doing less, being under committed instead of over committed. Drinking one glass of wine instead of two or three. Saying no to things that you don't want to do.

It can also mean consuming less, like resisting the urge to buy things at the store, especially if you're not going to use them right away or within the next 30 days. You can go into stores, admire things, think about them, and then not buy them!

Getting started is the hardest part, but give it a try!

Once you embrace minimalism, I believe that you will begin to have the life you have always dreamed of. You will have money in the bank. You will have peace in your home and your mind. You will have all of the time you would like for your projects, interests, and hobbies.

You will be able to read the book you're dying to read. You will be able to get out of town for the weekend. You will be able to sleep soundly, because when you go to bed at night, your mind won't be running furiously, giving you a list of things to do. Instead, you'll be able to drift right to sleep.

Minimalism Mantras:

I have less, and I gain more.

I am free with less.

I am committed to under-committing.

Saying no gives me freedom.

Getting rid of excuses and junk gives you a clear view of yourself. You might be surprised. We're often conscious of how we treat others. However, similar to being blind to all the junk we accumulate, we can be blind to how we treat ourselves.

Looking Inside Out

I know that we want to say that looks don't matter, but they do. How we look makes a first impression on everyone we meet. It's a reflection of ourselves.

People have strong opinions about this, especially about not caring what other people think. However, for better or worse, people do treat us how they see us. I'm not saying that it *should* be this way, rather it simply *is* that way.

A lot of us lawyers do not take proper care of ourselves. Our self-care is lacking and it shows. We wear faded, old clothes, worn down shoes, or come to work looking unkempt. Oftentimes we justify this by saying we are professionals and our work doesn't depend on our appearance. While that is true, the reality is that our appearance makes an impression and that impression is important.

It's easy to justify and hard to see the real reason

However, as I started doing deep work on myself, I realized that my attitudes about my old clothes reflected a deeply held, very painful belief that I was not worthy. That I didn't deserve something better. And that, perhaps, it was a way to test people to see if they really found me worthy.

That was the real reason, buried under so many justifications:

- I am busy.

- I don't have time to go shopping.

- I don't need anything new- my old things are perfectly fine.

- It takes too much time to dress up every single day to look my best.

- I have kids so I have other things to do.

- I am not vain like those glamorous office women, so I didn't need to do my hair and makeup.

- I am not shallow.

- I am an *intellectual*—someone who values education and travel over personal looks.

Sometimes our external looks are a reflection of what's going on inside

Be honest with yourself—how do you feel when you look your best? When you have your hair and makeup on point, when you have on clothes that make you feel beautiful and even sexy, when you have shoes that you love?

I'm willing to bet you feel powerful. You feel unstoppable. You feel on top of the world.

My question then is, what holds you back from trying to be your best self every single day?

The justifications we have-- they're all true: Being a mom is hard, being a lawyer is hard, running a business while doing both sometimes feels impossible. I completely get it.

But what if our external looks were a result of our internal condition? Maybe we feel run down, depleted, and overwhelmed and we let our exterior show that. Why not start with making ourselves feel amazing and let that really simmer and sink in.

Does your resistance to looking good come from self-doubt?

You are your harshest critic. I am sharing this with you, because I want you to know that I have struggled with making myself look "pulled together," and I think that a lot of us do.

Don't get me wrong, I am not saying that in order to be worthy or beautiful you have to have perfect hair or makeup.

What I am saying is that a lot of us resist trying to do these things because of **an incorrect belief that we are *not* worthy or beautiful or deserving, and as a result, we settle for a look that does not make us feel our best.**

My challenge to you is to go deep within yourself and your belief system.

- What stories are you telling yourself about your beauty and your worth?

- If you're in a rut, ask yourself what's holding you there.

- If you find that you have an old story or negative self-talk that is not true, allow yourself to change the story.

Start with self-love this second

Begin to shower yourself with love and compliments. Talk to yourself the way you'd talk to your daughter, your best friend, your sister, or your mother.

Experiment with looks that help you feel like the best version of yourself—little things here or there that help you unlock the highest level of power and confidence within you.

If you don't know where to start, you can try flipping through magazines. They have a lot of ideas on outfits and accessories. You can also work with a personal stylist for clothes.

Ask your hairdresser to teach you how to style your hair. Go to a makeup counter to ask for them to teach you how to achieve a makeup look you like. Watch Youtube video tutorials too. There are lots of good resources for easy hairstyles and makeup techniques for that everyday "natural but flawless" look.

Honor yourself. You are an amazing person. There is no one in the world like you. You deserve to feel your best. The world needs you to bring your best self forward.

Looking Inside Out Mantras:

I am beautiful. I am worthy. I am powerful.

I deserve inner and outer beauty.

The goal of looking good and feeling good is to allow your best self to come forward, it is *not* about holding yourself to an unrealistic standard of perfection. Chasing perfectionism is a way to rip joy from your life. It holds you back from success.

Beating Perfectionism

Perfectionism is one of the worst afflictions lawyers suffer. From applying for law school to graduating from it, we are groomed to strive to be the best.

After all, you make one mistake in a case, even an innocent mistake, and you risk getting a bar complaint. You could lose your entire livelihood by not being perfect!

Being a lawyer, that's just the way things are.

Add that to our type-A personalities and society's way of raising women to compete with one another over who is more perfect, and you have an entire industry of lawyers who are toiling to obtain the unattainable "perfection" in every way.

Perfection is a fake standard

I teach how to maximize efficiency in law firms, and one of the main ways is to delegate tasks—meaning you have to let go of the reins of some things.

I have had lawyers tell me that they value perfection over efficiency so they will only put out cases when they are 100% perfect, and that's why they have to prepare them themselves. They really believe perfection is an ideal and attainable goal.

But it's not. **Perfection is a fake standard. An impossible standard.** There is not one lawyer in the world who can prepare a case without one mistake. Yes, you can fix it before submitting, but mistakes happen.

Perfection should not be the goal

In addition to being impossible to achieve, it's actually a hindrance to success.

Perfectionism is something that affects women even more profoundly than men. Studies have shown that men will put out an idea, theory, or product that is decidedly not perfect. They will even say they don't have all the details figured out and still release something that provides the gist of their idea.

On the other hand, women will hold back. They only release something when they think it's been perfected. And since perfection is an unattainable standard, women often don't release things as quickly or take action because they believe it isn't perfect enough.

You can see where choosing not to act puts us at a disadvantage, along with the pressure to obtain an unrealistic standard.

Perfectionism holds you back

Sheryl Sandberg says, "Done is better than perfect."

In perfectionism, we create something, write something, or prepare something great or excellent, and instead of moving forward from that point to create the next great or excellent thing, we stay where we are and put in tons more effort to get our work to the level of "perfect."

For example, you write a great or excellent brief. But then you mull for hours over a small word choice that makes no large impact or the flow of the arguments, when the arguments are all made and made well.

In those hours you've wasted trying to "perfect" the brief, you could have written an entirely new one!

Don't look for acceptance from others

Perfectionism is essentially seeking external validation. You are looking outside yourself for approval, acceptance, and acknowledgment.

However, when we look outside ourselves for that approval and love, we are usually sorely disappointed. The only way we can gain peace is to work within ourselves to remove the misbelief that there is such a thing as perfectionism. We need to look inside ourselves and challenge ourselves to do our best—knowing that our best is going to be less than perfect.

Define what "your best" means

We have to define what "our best" means to us and to align it with our values. For example, I value efficiency very highly in my firm. Sometimes, efficiency does sacrifice the highest quality in order to get things done.

To give you an idea, we don't wait for inessential details in our forms. We just fill it in with "unknown" if the client can't immediately fill it in. We let it go and submit the case as quickly as possible.

Perfectionism would opt to wait, and it would likely cause a delay of a couple weeks, all for the sake of an insignificant piece of information.

Quality and perfection are not synonymous

It doesn't make sense to stick so strictly to perfection that we end up sacrificing efficiency and quality.

You see how I differentiate between perfection and quality?

People often mistakenly think the two are the same or similar words. They're not.

A high- quality work product or a perfect work product: When you put them next to each other like that, it's clear how different they are.

High quality and perfect aren't the same. High quality isn't aiming to be perfect—it just means that work is being done and it's being done well. But the people behind the work aren't wasting time and effort to make the work "perfect" because there is no return or additional gain from it.

Your peers are too busy trying for perfection themselves to scrutinize your work. Even if they do, who cares?

Many of us live with this constant quest for perfection because we fear what other lawyers will say if they ever see our work. The truth is, in most cases, other lawyers will never see your work. And even if they do, who cares?

If you are doing high-quality work, what does it matter? Additionally, we lawyers all have our different ways of doing things. Two lawyers may assemble the same type of case differently. It doesn't mean one is right and one is wrong. Rather, it just means that there are two ways to achieve the same end goal.

Perfection is not real

Let's be committed to letting go of perfectionism in every single area of our lives. Let's be willing to see that perfection is not real, and perfectionism is a hindrance to our success. Let's release our desire to be "perfect" today.

Perfectionism Mantra:

I release the need to be perfect.

My high-quality work is enough.

I am enough just as I am.

The wonderful thing about letting go of perfectionism is you free up your time. When you let go of the little things, you can finally focus on the big picture: your firm and its current success... or lack of success.

And because of all the realignment you've done to your mindset, your eyes are suddenly wide open. You realize you're earning below. And you deserve better. Much better.

Rising Above Earning Below

A lot of earning below comes from our incorrect belief that we shouldn't charge a lot for life-changing work. We think that because our work "makes things right," then it would be wrong to charge.

This is especially true when our clients are low income. We don't want to charge high prices—and sometimes we do not want to charge anything at all. We believe that the system is skewed against our clients. So in turn we believe we are righting a wrong with our work, and we shouldn't charge for it.

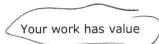
Your work has value

It's an important mindset shift for you to understand that doing great work in exchange for great money is a value-exchange.

Charging a price that reflects the value of your work isn't "stealing" or "being all about the money." It's simply demonstrating the value of the incredible work you do.

Both you and your clients benefit from an appropriate exchange of value. You both gain financial security, maintain work security, and can provide a high-quality life for your families.

In my work helping attorneys build the firms and lives of their dreams, and from my own experiences underearning, I've come up with four main categories in which we *earn below*.

Four Categories of "Earning Below"

1. Perception of a Client's Situation

We create perceptions of a client's financial situation before we actually know anything about it. I can't tell you how many times I have thought I should cut my fee because my client "can't afford it", and then found that the client's tax returns showed that he was earning more than I was!

Do great work and charge the right price for it

It is for a client to decide what he can and cannot afford, not you. Your job is to do great work and set an appropriate price for it.

You negotiate against yourself when you begin slashing fees because of what you think the client can or cannot afford.

You don't know what the client will or won't do

We also can't cut our prices to try to steer clients away from getting bad legal advice or the wrong legal service. Cutting our prices doesn't even mean that they won't go to the other place anyway!

This is a rationale I used myself to justify cutting my prices, then I was surprised when I heard other lawyers tell me that they were doing the same.

2. Devaluation of Our Work

We devalue the great work we do by undercharging, undercutting prices (even on prices that are already too low), and negotiating against ourselves to lower prices—oftentimes without a client even asking. We think that our work is "easy" so we do not need to charge more for it.

We also devalue our work when we don't charge for the extra work we end up doing in case, especially if we believe that the reason for the extra work is because something was "unfair" or not the client's fault.

We can absolutely make a healthy living while doing work that makes a difference. Loving your work and earning good money is not a mutually exclusive proposition.

3. Righting a Wrong By Cutting Fees

Sadly, we can't fix the unfairness of the system or unjust acts by charging the client less. We can fix any injustices by doing excellent work for our client—preferably at a price that reflects the value exchange: You provide a valuable service to the client, and the client pays you an appropriate value for that service.

Your client does not need your sympathy. Your client needs your expertise, hard work, and dedication. And the client is probably more than willing to pay what it takes for you to be the advocate she needs in order to make things right for her.

4. Being an Associate Instead of a CEO

I often hear the owners of law firms say that they "hate the business stuff." And I used to feel the same way. If that sentiment rings true for you, then you are likely acting like an associate in your law firm instead of the CEO.

If you want to "just do the work" and nothing else, it will be hard to do the work that you love, because you have to make a living doing it. If you don't take time to do or focus on the business stuff, then you are going to be overwhelmed.

Send a bill and get paid

Billing is key as the CEO of your law firm. One of the biggest reasons firms earn below is that they fail to bill. We often waive fees for costs of "small" case-related expenses.

But every dollar adds up. And I have learned the hard way: If you send a bill, you get paid. If you don't send a bill, you don't get paid. This is huge. You don't want to lose money each month because you fail to bill or fail to bill properly.

Maximize with efficiency

Inefficiency and disorganization in the firm—whether it is hard files, e-files, or financial disorganization—will affect your bottom line.

Getting files organized is important whether you are a law firm owner or an associate because it will help things run more smoothly. Thirty minutes looking for a paper mislabeled, not filed, or not saved in a consistent procedure is thirty minutes wasted.

On the other hand, simple steps— like maximizing a sign up to get started on a case instead of chasing down a client after they have signed a contract—will make a huge difference to your law firm.

Know your finances

An associate doesn't know her firm's finances. A CEO does and should. Being in the dark about your firm's finances will throw the entire firm into financial chaos and will affect every member of the firm.

Regardless of how scary it is, turn on the light. See what's there. Know your expenses every month. Know when each bill is due. Know how much is coming in each month—how many people are on payment plans, how many people paid in full, how much is coming in new contracts and consults.

Knowing your law firm's numbers will make all the difference. You'll be able to set benchmarks, track your earnings, set goals, and eventually earn more!

Being aware of how and why you're earning below should realign your mindset and jumpstart a more profitable, much happier career. Instead of overwhelm, you'll have information and efficiency. Instead of earning below, you'll earn more money and your perspective will opens up.

All the sections in this chapter about Mindset should result in a new you. You will no longer be buried with the day-to-day struggles of your firm. Instead, your mind will be looking straight ahead to strategize for continuing success.

Workbook

Now it's your turn! Go to page 1 of the Workbook and fill out the exercises for Chapter 1. Visit: http://bit.ly/LFBS-Book

Chapter 2: Vision and Strategy

Without vision and strategy to acheive it, you're not really a CEO of your law firm. You're "just doing the job," going through day-to-day activities for your firm like an associate instead of a CEO.

Vision gives you goals. Strategy is your gameplan to achieve those goals as efficiently as possible.

The Firm and Life of Your Dreams

I am going to tell you something that you may find shocking. **Your law firm exists for *you*.**

It doesn't exist for your clients or for your staff. The reason that a law firm exists is so that you can do the work that you love to do and earn money for doing it. That's it.

You serve your clients and you give your staff jobs. But a law firm is a business. And every business exists to make money for its owners.

Most of us don't think of our law firms as businesses— instead we see them as the vehicle through which we can do legal work. What happens then is that we neglect the business side of things to focus on doing our work.

One cannot exist without the other. You need to run your firm like a business, and of course you need to do excellent work to keep doing business!

Now let me tell you something else. **You can have the life of your dreams through your law firm.**

This may be hard to imagine if you're currently working non-stop, feeling constantly overwhelmed, waking up in the middle of the night stressed out, and thinking that your law firm would implode if you took a much-needed vacation.

I understand the feeling 100%, and I have been there before.

But it IS possible to have your law firm give you the most incredible life. *The first step is realizing that it is possible.*

You have to look at the law firm like the owner of a business instead of like an associate attorney working in the firm. When you start to view the law firm this way, you will start to be able to embrace the idea that you can make your firm work for you.

Your firm should work for you

Your law firm needs to provide some of the biggest things you want for your life: money, stability, happiness.

- Do you want to take a week-long vacation every month?

- Do you want to work 20-hour work weeks?

- Do you want to be able to have an amazing night's sleep where you never once wake up stressing out over work, thinking that you forgot something, or fearing that something slipped through the cracks?

Decide what you want for your life. And then use your law firm as a way to get it.

We aren't talking about something that's slimy, sleazy, or taking advantage of people. We are talking about doing excellent work from which you make an excellent living.

Define success in your own way. Then create the law firm that meets that definition.

No one would define success as 60-80 hour workweeks without vacation or time for yourself and your family!

I want you to think of your law firm differently. I want you to see that you can have the law firm and life of your dreams. All you need to do is start thinking differently. First of all, what do you want from your law firm?

Determining What You Want Out Of Your Law Firm

Determine the type of life you want and the type of firm you want.

This is the vision of your law firm and your life. I want to help you put it all into words.

This is going to be an interactive lesson. I encourage you to respond to the prompts as we go along.

<u>Personal Life</u>

The 5 most important things to me in my life are:

3 things I wish I did more of:

3 things I wish I did less of:

How do I want to feel every single day?

What do I want to achieve in the next 365 days?

What do I want to achieve in the next 5 years?

What do I want to achieve in the next decade of my life?

What is a huge, big, audacious goal I have? (Maybe one that I haven't told anymore—or only told a few people)

My dream life looks like: (house, car, neighborhood, daily activities, travel, schools, etc)

What are 3 things that I can do right now to improve the quality of my life?

<u>Professional Life</u>

If I had to do one case type only for the rest of my career, what would it be?

Who are the clients I would like to serve?

How many hours do I want to work a year?

How many vacations would I like to take in the next year?

How much money do I want to earn a year? (think BIG!)

Take that number and double it.

What are the benchmarks for that amount by month and by week? (i.e. $1M a year is $83,333 a month, and about $20,000 week)

What are my 3 biggest professional goals?

What would I like to achieve in the next 3 months?

What would I like to achieve in the next 6 months?

What would I like to achieve in the next 12 months?

What are 3 steps that I can take to improve my business today?

What are 3 ways that I can make my law firm work *for* me instead of me working for my law firm? (i.e. working set, fixed hours instead of being always "on")

Take the time to write this all down. It's powerful to put it in writing. It supercharges your dreams.

As you do this, don't feel like you have to be perfect or literal. Feel free to take whatever pops into your head and put it into words.

I know that sometimes we hesitate writing things down, because we feel like we have to know how we are going to achieve a goal to be able to hold the goal. But you don't have to figure out the *how*. Not right now.

Once you start thinking about the results you want as if they were already achieved, then the ways to get there will begin to open before you. Stay focused on your goals and don't get distracted.

Branding and Marketing

A big part of turning your firm into your dream firm is branding and marketing. Lawyers think branding and marketing are dirty words. We think that if we loved our work, we wouldn't need to "brand" or "market" ourselves. Or even worse, we fall into the false belief that if we were good enough lawyers, we wouldn't need marketing.

It is so frustrating when you are a new or struggling solo and you ask an attorney for advice on how they get the majority of business, and they say, "Do great work and you will get referrals."

Well, obviously. However, when you are just starting out and looking to build up your practice—or even when you are established and want to grow your practice—you need to get the word out that you are here, and you are ready to represent clients.

Your personal brand

Your personal brand lets your clients know who you are, what you do, why you do it, and why you are different.

People need your services. If you don't see your law firm as a brand, and if you don't establish a personal brand, you lose visibility.

You and your firm stand for something. You became a lawyer because you believed in something. You do the area of law you specialize in for a specific, personal reasons.

So why would your law firm look like a cookie-cutter copy of every other law firm out there?

A brand is comprised of three parts:

1. Tagline

2. Logo

3. Professional Photo

When you put together your brand, remember **this is about your *Ideal Client*, not about you**. At all. Ask yourself, "What would my Ideal Client like to see/ hear/ know from me?"

This comes out in your tagline, logo, and professional photo.

Your Tagline

A tagline is one sentence or a sentence fragment that sums up what you do in a way that touches the pain points of your Ideal Client.

- Your clients have problems or situations that need solutions.

- And they need to know that you are the right person for the job.

A lot of us fall short because we are used to the cookie-cutter way lawyers express things, like *"Justice For You."*

Who is the justice for? And why? Have you been wrongfully imprisoned for 10 years and now you need justice? Or are you fighting against an unfair traffic ticket? The tagline is useless to help the client understand what you do and who you serve.

Examples of good taglines:

- "Uniting families through the use of the U.S. immigration system."

- "Helping entrepreneurs achieve their dreams by protecting their intellectual property."

Your tagline should be specific and tailored to your Ideal Client and their pain points.

Your Logo

Ditch the usual scales of justice and get something that represents you and your firm.

Logo and graphic design service websites can do this for you cheaply, for about $100. By using a logo company, you'll be able to get a logo in several digital formats so that you can easily upload it to your website, use it on your social media, and have it printed on your business cards.

Remember, these are investments in your legal business, not merely expenses.

I have really enjoyed working with Conception Logo which charges about $100 and they create 3 different logos for you and will tailor these to your ideas and likes/dislikes until you get the perfect logo for your law firm.

How to nail your firm's logo:

- Reflect on your Ideal Client, your tagline, and what your firm represents.

- Go for a strong symbol to show what your firm stands for.

- What would your Ideal Client like? What would they remember? What would make an impact on them?

For example, I serve the Mexican community almost exclusively, so I picked an important symbol from Mexican culture, used the colors of the Mexican flag, and incorporated my law firm's name into it. My clients comment on the logo all of the time. It's very recognizable for them.

Your logo is an opportunity to show your self-expression. Part of your homework this chapter is to create a logo for your law firm.

Your Professional Photo

Non-negotiable: you must have a professional photo to tie together your professional image and to unite your online platforms. This is an investment, and it makes a huge difference. You can see my professional photo on my websites, and it unifies my brand.

More homework for you: Find a photographer and schedule an appointment for your professional photo.

Ladies, see if you can find a photographer who offers a hair and makeup package. Or go to your favorite salon for a special styling and makeup for the shoot. I have found that service to run an additional $150.00 or so.

Now that you have taken steps to establish your personal brand, the next step is to attach success to your brand!

Think Creatively About Success

Break free from the hourly billing model! I want you to think creatively about ways that you can create more income while you do great work.

Here are the numbers:

To earn $500,000 a year:

- You only need 96 clients in a year who pay $5200 for a case.

- That's only 8 clients a month.

In order to earn $1,000,000 a year:

- You only need 116 clients in a year who pay $8600 for a case.

- That's only 9 clients a month.

These numbers are COMPLETELY DOABLE! This is not out of reach at all.

When I realized that this was the breakdown, I decided I would price all of my cases differently. I decided that I could earn this fee by doing excellent, fast work.

Clients love it

I knew that the price of $8600 (well, we actually charge $8500 per case) was something my clients would pay if I could deliver big value to them. My work changes lives, and so does yours.

I focused on the value that a positive outcome would bring, plus my unique way of doing things, and I was able to adjust my services to make it worth every cent to clients.

My all-inclusive legal fee

- Clients hated that they were "constantly being charged" for additional things.

- They wanted a price that included everything.

- They didn't ever want to pay another cent than what they were told.

That's when I came up with the idea of an "all-inclusive legal fee" where I stopped bifurcating work and stopped leaving things out or charging separately for everything. I decided that I would include every single thing in my fee, every contingency, everything. I decided not to charge separately for anything.

And CLIENTS LOVE IT!

When all is said and done, the $8500 fee just *sounds* higher. It actually isn't higher. I just charge everything from the beginning and don't charge anything later.

Two interesting things you'll soon notice:

- When we are stuck in underearning, we usually break up the different things that the clients have to pay for. Here's the rub- oftentimes we don't charge them for it after all. We also fail to charge when we do extra work. That means that by not contemplating all of the "extras" that go into every case, you are essentially slashing all of your fees even more.

- When we charge a higher fee from the beginning, we begin to insulate ourselves from the trap of underearning. It's almost like we are saving ourselves from ourselves—we set ourselves up to succeed.

Let's talk about some other creative ways that you can make money through your law firm:

Webinars

- Free webinars: In a free webinar you can address common questions that you receive to get people to view the webinar. During the webinar, you will "sell" your services as you go. You'll give great info, so people can watch and feel informed. But they'll likely also be left feeling motivated to get moving with hiring you to do their estate plan.

- Paid webinars: They can be live or pre-recorded. During the paid webinar you give specific information about a particular topic. If you serve a population that has a lot of "do-it-yourselfers," they will likely love a webinar.

    o Record it, and then forget it. It's on your website for sale. People looking around your site can buy the webinar. Maybe they will take it and run with it and do the work themselves, or maybe they will realize that they have more questions than they thought. Either way, you will be able to earn money from the webinar, establish yourself as an expert, and build your business!

Legal Packages

This is work you already do just presented in a different, client-centric way. Here are some examples:

- Startup package: covers all filings that a new business needs in order to get up and going.

- Quickie divorce package: uncontested divorces, little to no assets and no children

Put it on your website, or as part of a menu you offer when clients consult online or in person. Make sure you also have it printed and prepared for those who visit your office so you can "pitch" it to them while in a consultation.

Subscription Services

Subscription services are genius. They serve the needs of your clients, and they are a great guaranteed income for you.

A subscription service is just like a gym membership: You pay for it, and you maximize it; or you pay for it, and you barely use it.

- a flat fee that covers hours, questions, or services

- paid whether the client uses every second of the time available to them or not

- perfect for lawyers with clients who often have follow-up questions after a matter has ended—like divorces where the clients have follow-up questions about custody, or employment law where clients consult about various HR questions

E-Books

An e-book is a great way to show your expertise, set you apart from others, and enable you to earn income. E-books don't have to be long. They can be about 20 pages. You can do the whole thing with very little time and money.

- Put together an outline and some notes, and then and then hire a ghostwriter. You get a draft, you edit, and voila! You have a book.

- Outsource the cover design and formatting.

- Make it available on your website, either for free with the intent of gathering leads, or priced with "an exclusive discount." Either way will make you more money.

These ideas should get your creativity flowing on how to serve your clients and make money in different ways. You should definitely see by now that you *can* make your law firm work for you.

Keep your eyes on the prize—maintain a CEO mindset—instead of allowing yourself to become an associate again. It's all about vision and strategy.

Workbook

Now it's your turn! Go to page 4 of the Workbook and fill out the exercises for Chapter 1. Visit: http://bit.ly/LFBS-Book

Chapter Three: Finances

You need to get your finances in order. It is crucial for your survival. If you want to keep doing the work you love, you need financial structure and success.

I know figuring out your finances can be extremely stressful and overwhelming. (I even would call it scary.) Most lawyers would agree, saying that we're bad at numbers and we just "want to do the work.". How we got the reputation for being money hungry is something I will never understand, because most of us are underearning and don't have a clue about how our finances are going!

Can you answer these questions with certainty?

- Do you know how much money is coming into your firm each month?

- Do you know how much money is coming into your firm each week?

- Do you know every single set expense in your firm?

- Do you know on which date all of your payments are due?

- Do you overdraw your account?

- Do you overdraw your account regularly?

- Do you feel afraid each month that you aren't going to make it?

- Do you avoid paying yourself a salary because you feel like you can't afford it?

- Do you feel embarrassed or ashamed because of the state of the finances in your law firm?

I couldn't answer those questions with any certainty before. I used to be in financial chaos.

- I overdrew my account at least once a month, sometimes more.

- I had no idea how much was coming in or coming out.

- I paid my bills late, because I had their due dates disorganized.

- I didn't send bills or receipts to clients, so I didn't know who owed what or who had paid what.

- I didn't know if people were paying on time or if bills were paid.

If you're in that place right now, it's OKAY! You can get out of it! You can get your finances in order, slowly but surely, by taking small—but significant—steps in the right direction.

Know Your Expenses

You need to know your "breakeven point." That is the amount that you *have* to earn in order to pay for everything you need to continue running your firm.

- Your salary and payroll: You must, must, must pay yourself a salary.

- Rent/mortgage payments on your office

- Utilities and services: everything essential to running your firm, like your case management system, your IT/phone answering services, etc.

- Mailing costs

- ---include list of expenses mentioned in script here---

It's up to you whether you do it alone or not, but get it done.

If you need professional assistance, that doesn't mean that you have failed or that you are dumb or that you aren't good enough. Instead, it means you care about your business and doing the absolute best for yourself and your clients. Getting your finances in order is also a service to your clients.

Costs vs Investments

Costs drain away money without returns while investments offer returns. Each one of the items on your Expenses list should be essential to running your business, giving you the ability to do the work you love, serve your clients, and use your law degree to its fullest.

Here are some of the services and products you pay for that are investments into your business:

- Bench bookkeeping

- Your case management system

- Your phone answering service

- Your staff and your salary

- Your mailing costs

As you grow, your needs grow. You need to invest in better technology and equipment. Part of getting your finances in order is identifying how to invest smartly.

- Hiring more people/outsourcing to experts

- Switching to better service providers

- Investing in office machines/products and online tools that save you and your staff time

All of these are sound investments for your continued success.

Don't settle for "good enough." It's a trap that we set for ourselves and it prevents us from setting ourselves up to succeed. If we keep clinging to old ways of thinking and doing, we are limiting our success.

Money isn't the only precious resource in your law firm. There's also time. Efficiency is key. Investing in something new can save you time—whether it's the right scanner, a new case management system, or a new staff member such as a business manager or an administrative assistant.

Consider the financial investment and financial return. *And* consider the return on your time, which is the most important and irreplaceable asset.

Instead of thinking about how much that new Scansnap would cost, focus on how much you will gain in time for your team to work on more cases in a day because they won't constantly be waiting around for the old, outdated scanner.

Focus on revenues

A lot of law firms already try to keep expenses low, so I won't start by telling you to cut down expenses. Don't get lost in trying to cut expenses. Instead, **spend your time and energy on finding ways to increase revenues!**

The most important line on your Profit and Loss statement is your PROFIT line. You need to make more money. Now. Everyday. You need to make money.

I am not saying to go on a spending spree and to ignore your expenses all together. Absolutely not. I just don't want you to waste your precious time and energy trying to squeeze every last drop of juice out of your expenses. Instead, I want you to maximize your time and energy by building your business—bring in new clients, find ways to do more for existing clients, and bring back old clients for some repeat business.

Once you know your breakeven point, get down to the most important work in your firm: your clients. Get more, make more, do more, enjoy more. It's really that simple!

Stop Using These Useless and Potentially Damaging Penny-Pinching Tactics NOW!

Here are some things that I want you to stop doing in your law firm right now.

- **Paying business expenses with your personal credit cards**. Get a credit card for your firm and use that. Mixing expenses is very confusing come tax season, and the last thing that you need is an audit! You have enough other things to do with your time.

- **Doing your own bookkeeping.** Be a lawyer, hire a bookkeeper. I always recommend Bench, which is a virtual bookkeeping service. You have a virtual bookkeeper who you can call, email, and message as much as you would like, or you can just let her do her thing while you are busy doing legal work. I love them so much that I partnered with them. You get a free month *and* 20% off the first 6 months of your service when you call and ask for the Ally Lozano discount.

- **Trying to do everything yourself.** You can't. Hire someone to help you in the office, even if it is a few hours a week. As scary as it is to invest in having in-office help, once you do it, you will ask yourself why you didn't do it sooner.

- **Refusing to pay yourself a salary.** It is ESSENTIAL that you pay yourself a salary, even if you feel like you can't afford it. When there's money in the bank, it will get spent somehow. Start with your salary. You should get paid for your hard work! Pay yourself. Today. I love Gusto for payroll. They make things super easy.

- **Avoiding your bank account.** You need to look at it. Know what's there, what's coming in, and what's flowing out. Check it. Care for it. Nurture it. In order to do the work that you love, you have to have a healthy bank account.

- **Failing to send bills.** If you send bills, you get paid. If you don't, you don't. Keep track of who has paid, how much they have paid, and how much they owe. Once you get going with it, you'll find it is easier than you thought! You also need to know who isn't paying, so that you can get that client on track, or send him to collections.

Credit Cards

Another option to consider when it comes to finances is credit cards. Something many small businesses struggle with, not just law firms, is that they refuse to accept credit cards. These are the fears when it comes to accepting credit cards:

- The credit card processing fee might be too high, and it will eat away at profits.

- Some states don't allow businesses to charge a credit card processing fee, so some businesses feel like they will take too much of a hit to their bottom line revenues.

- With increased credit card processing, there will be increased tax liability.

I had these fears. BUT within one month of accepting credit cards, my income doubled. Also, I found out that all of those fees the credit card processing company charged were tax write offs, yet I was scared that it would actually cause me to pay *more* taxes. Credit cards will revolutionize your business. Start accepting them today.

How to minimize costs and maximize revenue when you accept credit cards

1. Compare different credit card processors. This can be overwhelming. If you don't have time, just pick one, and go with it. Accepting credit cards today is better than waiting to find the perfect credit card processor two months from now. If you can't get the estimates now, start accepting credit cards anyway. You can even start with something like Square. Do it *right now*.

Two things you'll discover:

- Credit card processing companies compete for your business. A lot of them will offer a comparison of your current rates vs. their rates.

- Your rate is usually determined by how many transactions you have each month and the average cost of the transactions. The more transactions you have and the higher-value they are, the more discounts the credit card processors provide.

2. Check in every 6-12 months to make sure that you're maximizing your discounts and that the rates you are getting are the most competitive out there. This is an easy way for you to make sure that more of your money goes directly to you.

3. Set up Automatic Payments. Set it, and forget it, and you get paid every month. This takes away the huge job of creating bills, mailing bills, reminding the client that he needs to pay, following up about a late payment, threatening the client for a late payment, and more unpleasant things.

Our clients sign an authorization for an automatic debit of a certain amount on a certain date. Then we send a receipt each month showing a full accounting of what is left on the bill— and voila—it's done. It simplifies the entire system.

This one small step can help you earn significantly more while significantly decreasing your stress and workload.

4. Offer a cash price lower than the credit card price. Credit cards are a great convenience for the client, but they do have a small cost to you. Instead of passing credit card processing fees along to clients, you can incentivize them to pay with cash, check, cashier's check, etc, by giving them a lower price for your services if they pay without using a credit card.

5. Prepaid consultations. Once you accept credit cards, you can require prepaid consultations. This one move will bring your no-show rate down to zero. When consultations are prepaid, it ensures people will show up. This will make you more money, right now.

6. Collect payments through your website. Allow potential clients to schedule and pay for consultations directly through your website.Set up a payment link on your website where current clients can make a payment on an existing case. It's a fast and easy way to collect payment without them having to call your law firm.

7. Collect payments through your case management system.
Many case management systems allow clients to pay through a client portal. With a click of a button, you can send a bill that the client clicks to pay. As my kids say, it's "easy, peasy, lemon squeezy."

8. Create a PayPal account. A lot of people have PayPal. It's also a credit card processor, and while you can likely find cheaper ones, having PayPal in addition to other credit card processors provides multiple quick and easy options for your clients to pay you. That's the important thing: getting paid.

Consultation Conundrum

To charge or not to charge for consultations? That's a burning question for lawyers, and **yes you should charge for consultations.** With a credit card processor, you can now make pre-payment for consultations easy and quick.

Why You Should Charge for Consultations

Consultations are hugely important and they can make or break your business. Simply put: if you have no consultations, you have no business. Consultations bring in new clients and make you and your brand known to potential clients.

Because you know that you need consultations for your business to survive, you make feel like you need to do free consultations in order to get people in the door. Wrong.

Your knowledge has value.

Despite Googling her problem, posting in forums, reading books, and talking about it with other people, your client still needs to talk to you, a lawyer.

You're the expert. Even if there is no legal remedy for your client, she comes away with expert information and advice. The advice may include: what she qualifies for, what the next steps are, and what you need from her. Or, the advice may be that she does not seem to qualify for anything at the moment, and you'll help her understand the reasons why.

Your expertise comes from three years of law school and many years of experience as a lawyer, and that's not even counting the years in college.

There is so much value in having a lawyer evaluate a legal issue.

Your time has value.

In the 30-minute or one-hour consultation, you listen to a potential client, analyze her case, and give her legal advice. Your focus during that consultation is 100% on that client. You cannot do one other thing at that time.

Every time you do a consultation, you're unable to spend that time working for paying clients. You are taking away time from everything else. So you must value the time that you are reserving for the consultation.

Charging for consultations is a *must*.

Charging for consultations is a must to have a thriving practice. You increase revenues while, at the same time, ensuring that people who come to you aren't just "looky loos," those just looking to get information but aren't ready to act or don't want to pay.

Now that you've been convinced to charge for consults, let's talk about requiring pre-payment for consultations.

Requiring pre-payments for consultations

This is a game changer. If you don't require pre-payment, you'll likely have a high no-show rate. If you don't think that you do, track it. My no-show rate was at about 50% before I started requiring pre-payments. Now, it is at 0%.

Paying the consult fee in advance has so many advantages for you and your clients.

- You weed out the flakes and avoid the no-shows. Even with reminders, people just don't show up if they haven't paid for it.

- You prepare clients for paying attorney fees. If they won't even pay the consult fee, chances are they won't want to pay for your services at all. You want to attract people who are willing and able to invest in your services.

- Your client arrives at your firm and proceeds with the consult instead of taking the time and the steps to make a payment.

- You can create a cancellation that makes both parties comfortable. For example, if they cancel with 24-hour notice, then you will refund the payment. Easy.

A person canceling a consult is the exception, not the rule, so plan instead on them showing up.

This is a fast way to start making more money in your law firm today. At first it feels scary because you are probably used to your calendar being filled with consultations, even though a large percentage of them do not show up. Once you require pre-payment, your calendar will look a lot lighter. You may feel like you are losing new clients with this new policy. However, what is happening is that the people who were going to actually show up and pay are the ones who actually schedule.

How to do free consultations right

There is plenty of free legal information out there. It doesn't have to come from you. It is not your responsibility as an attorney to provide free legal information to anyone by way of a consultation.

You're running a business. You can't afford free consults that turn into nothing, because the clients you attract with free consults are people who aren't willing to invest in your fees at all.

BUT there are ways to do free consultations, serve the community, *and* make more money in your firm all at the same time.

1. A free legal clinic YOU host

By hosting a free clinic yourself, you get to help your local community, and it doubles as marketing for your law firm. Host it at your firm and brand it with your firm's branding. Promote it on social networks and connect with other leaders in the community: city/neighborhood newsletters, local radio show hosts, and so on.

For the clinic, be sure to have a process for the day-of, because if you get the word out in the right way, you are going to get a lot of people who show up.

- Prepare a very detailed intake sheet that people have to fill out when they show up so that you can quickly narrow the issues, since you won't be able to spend more than 15 minutes with the consults. I've had clinics where almost 100 people show up, and we have had to do 5-10 minute consults! You have to be prepared.

- Make sure that the language in the intake sheet indicates that you are *not* their lawyer absent the signing of a formal contract.

2. A call-in legal clinic

Hosting a call-in legal clinic is like hosting a call-in radio show. At a certain time on a certain date, people can call a certain number (a conference call number) and you will be there taking questions. Everyone can listen in and gain value without having to call themselves.

After a quick consult, when you see that you can help the caller, refer them to a full consult. Offer a discount if they call your office right that moment and schedule. This means that in addition to you being live on the conference call line, you need someone standing by at the office to handle the calls.

I use UberConference for my conference call line and I paid for a number that does not require a PIN when people call in. I usually schedule it for 6pm on a Sunday, and I'm available on the line only for 1 hour. I have generated, on average, $20,000, from these calls.

You can do it from home. You don't even have to get dressed up! It's one quick hour of your time! Well worth it!

3. A Facebook Live show

I love Facebook Live for my business. Create your own Facebook Live show and watch your business grow. Here's how you do it:

- Give your show a name.

- Make it a weekly show every week at the same time on the same day of the week (i.e. Mondays at 6pm).

- Use the show to answer people's questions live. Be sure to remind your watchers over and over to ask questions so you can answer them.

- Choose a topic to discuss while waiting for people to send in their questions. Make the topics focused around your main case types so you "sell" people on them.

- Don't get too technical or use too much legalese. Your viewers want to understand the benefits to them of the legal process, not the legal techniques that you are going to use to complete the process.

- Regardless of the question, use very general information to respond so that other people watching and listening can see how that advice applies to their situations as well.

- Do not give legal advice, it's just a forum to give general legal information. Remind your viewers of that. (And of course, always comply with your bar's ethics rules).

- Repeat your phone number over and over. It feels repetitive, but it isn't. Every time you answer a question, remind people that they can call in to your office to discuss their cases further.

- Remind people to share the video. (i.e. "Thanks for your question! Don't forget to share this video!")

- Make it fun! Keep your energy high and engaging. If it's a show, then people need to want to watch it. Plus, the more fun you make it, the more fun you will have.

Your Facebook Live show stays on your Facebook page for people to view—even if they didn't get to send in their questions. It's great visibility for your firm. And when people send specific questions, you can refer them to full consultations.

With these techniques, you can see that you can still do a lot of work educating the community and giving out free legal information while skipping free or underpaid consults. Your business can build goodwill under your name and brand while still profiting for you.

Remember, your time and expertise have value. If you are giving information for free, make sure that it has a benefit to you as much as it benefits the person receiving it.

Get Your Fees Right

Setting fees too low is one of the ways that lawyers get stuck in underearning.

I am a huge proponent of flat fees, but you need to set your flat fees right in order to make them work for you.

Why Use Flat Fees

The hourly rate system is completely outdated and, most damaging of all, it's inefficient. With hourly rates, if you want to make more money, you need to work more hours.

You are disincentivized from making your law firm efficient.

For example, in my streamlined law firm, this is what we have:

- Fully templated contracts, easy to use and put together

- Legal arguments that barely need any tailoring to the specific case other than inputting the client's facts

- Sign up processes that allow us to complete an entire case in a week or less

All the above have huge payoffs in efficiency, client satisfaction, and workload BUT have *zero* financial payoff if you are billing by the hour.

Hourly rates don't pay for efficiency. In fact, hourly billing is why we rarely see efficient law firms. You want to be streamlined and have a law firm that runs as efficiently as a car assembly line and as consistently as a Starbucks.

Let's look at the numbers here for a moment:

If you wanted to earn $1M a year and you bill at $350/ hour, if you take into consideration time off for holidays and vacation, giving you 48 working weeks a year, you would have to *bill* 59 hours a week. That doesn't mean *work* 59 hours a week. That means *billable work only*. Do you see how your earnings are capped by your labor? You are limited in what you can ever earn. It is nearly, if not completely, impossible to bill 59 hours a week of lawyer work.

Flat fees will change your life. You can get paid what a case is worth while having extremely fast turnaround times and an excellent work product. You can serve more people, make more money, and infinitely increase client satisfaction.

Set the Right Flat Fee

Flat fees only work if you set them correctly. For years I was stuck in underearning because I set the wrong flat fee. Now that I have correctly set my fees, I can tell you that I was underearning by *at least* $5,000 per case.

When setting a flat fee, do not look to other lawyer's fees and the "industry standard." Remember that most lawyers are underearning and you might just get stuck in the same cycle if you look to them as a model.

Home remodelers and contractors bid on projects, taking into account every single factor that may arise. This is what you should do and this is how you make flat fees work for you and your firm.

What to include in your flat fee:

- The legal work to be done

- Client communications

- Client hand-holding

- Foreseeable contingencies and issues that may come up

- Administrative fees

- And more

Not including these in your flat fee is bad because the client expects them from you. I've never met a lawyer who hasn't told clients they will be available for anything and everything the client needs as the case progresses.

Your fees and the efficiency of your firm should cover that and make that possible.

This is why everything that you do on a case from beginning to end should be included in the fee. I like to present an all-inclusive fee to my clients. The total of the admin fee and the flat fee of my cases. They know the "everything" price from the beginning.

As you do this, you'll discover it is easier than you thought, both for you and your clients. Your clients don't have to see a parade of bills in the mail—and you won't have to send any either, which just adds to the efficiency in your firm! And remember, more efficiency means more happy clients more clients served and more profits.

Get Paid in Full

Getting paid in full seems impossible for us lawyers.

I had never in my life ever quoted a fee in its entirety and then just left it like that. I immediately offered a payment plan the second that the price came out of my mouth. That is how I had been taught, so that is how I did it.

Finally, about a year ago, we were getting run down with the runaround of payment plans. While we had most people on automatic debit, there was still so much managing that was required in the payment plans.

So my husband and I sat down to brainstorm ideas, and he said that we need to reel in the payment plans to no more than 6 months and offer an incentive for people to pay in full. I completely balked at the idea. I thought there was no way people would pay in full. But I did like the idea of a case being paid off in no more than 6 months. What we came up with was a plan where a case would be $1000 cheaper if a person paid in full.

Armed with my new prices, I started quoting people the two tiers- pay in full, or for $1000 more, have a payment plan. What was incredible was that person after person after person selected to pay in full.

I couldn't believe it.

iQualify

This is another game changer. If you are offering payment plans to clients, you are essentially acting as a bank. You are giving someone credit from your law firm to pay for your legal services. You are offering them a payment plan based on their word alone that they will pay you. It's time to stop being a bank and leave the payment issues to someone else. That's where iQualify comes in.

iQualify offers financing for legal cases so that people can afford legal services *and* help lawyers pay in full for legal cases. Any payments for financing are made with iQualify directly, which means that you are completely off the hook for collecting payments. All of this is done at the fraction of what it would cost to have a full-time person in your law firm trying to manage all of your billing and receivables.

If your client doesn't qualify for loan through iQualify for the full amount of your legal services, iQualify can *manage and collect on the payment plan for you.* Talk about revolutionary!

Your success is going to skyrocket. You'll be making more money and getting paid in full. And if clients can't pay in full, you get paid without ever having to worry about sending a bill, because the iQualify team will handle that for you.

I have partnered with iQualify because I believe in the product. I believe lawyers can do better work if they are paid properly and are not forced to use scarce resources to collect payments. I also believe in their mission of helping people access legal services who may not otherwise be able to afford them. If you decide to use iQualify, there is an "Ally Lozano" discount, so be sure to mention it. You will be glad that you did!

With flat fees, paid consults, full payments, and iQualify, you're well on your way to a successful, profitable law firm!

But what about pro bono work, then?

Pro Bono Work

Here's the problem that most small and solo firms face: pro bono work doesn't usually start out as pro bono work. Things in the case can take an unexpected turn and you fail or refuse to charge more. This usually happens when we feel bad about the situation, when we feel bad about an injustice, or when we feel bad about the client's life circumstances.

We are human and of course we do not want people to suffer and we do not want injustices to go uncured. But we are also business people who are running businesses, so we must behave that way. And pro bono and low bono are not successful business models. They are what nonprofits are made for. I used to run my for-profit firm like a nonprofit, so I completely understand how easy it is to keep falling into this and keep yourself stuck in an underearning cycle.

I want to help you be very purposeful about your selection of pro bono work so you do *intentional* pro bono work instead of constantly doing it on accident.

1. At the beginning of the year, or at the beginning of each quarter, determine how many pro bono and/or low bono cases you will take. Take into consideration the types of cases you are willing to take on low or pro bono given the time commitment and resources that are required to make them happen. This will help you be selective about cutting your fees or not charging when a particularly sympathetic case presents itself to you.

2. Make a commitment to only accept pro bono cases through specific non-profits. This takes #1 to the next level, because it forces you to not take any pro bono through your firm. This allows you to honor your commitment to pro bono through cases that are selected by someone else. This means that you will not ever be in a consultation and offer to do the case completely for free. It won't be possible, because you will have committed to only take pro bono cases through an agency.

3. Have a "pro bono running buddy" who will help hold you accountable. Before you offer to do a case for free, or before you offer to cut a fee, put a "check" on yourself: Assign yourself a person that you have to ask permission from before cutting any fee. For me, it's my business manager. And since he says, "no," so often, I am extremely selective about cases I will even consider bringing to him and asking to do on a discount. It is really important to have this accountability because if you are left to your own devices you will cut the fee and not think twice. This is something I would still do if I were left to my own devices. So make sure that you have someone to "ask" to give you the yes or no. Be sure to pick someone who won't have "yes" as their default!!

4. Create a pro bono and low bono referral list. If a client is insistent that he can't pay, provide him with a list of other attorneys he can call who might work with his particular circumstances on a low bono or pro bono basis.

It took a long time for me to break my low bono, pro bono, underearning mindset, but now that I have, I know that I will never go back.

I value my time and services so much more now. I consider my quarterly free legal clinics and my weekly Facebook Live shows my pro bono work. I love doing both of those things and I know that my community is better as a result of the free work I do. Pro bono can be wonderful when it's done right, but if done wrong, it's draining for you and your firm.

The Type of Law Firm You Want To Be

We want to be great lawyers. We want to do excellent work. We want to give our clients the results that they desire. We want to fight for justice and the rule of law. We want to show up each day and do our best.

However, many of us have never given thought to the type of law firm that we want to be. For example, do you want to be Walmart or Neiman Marcus or something in between?

Walmart's business model is having the lowest price. This is where we set our fees based on the market or what we know other lawyers charge. We believe that people won't hire us unless we offer the "going rate" or less.

Here's the thing: most clients don't know what other people charge. It's just a story we have made up in our minds to justify undercharging and underearning.

Instead of focusing on what others are doing, focus on what it is that you do, how you want to do it better, and what you do that is different.

Determine whether you want your firm to be Walmart or Neiman Marcus. That will help you figure things out.

As Walmart:

- You need a higher volume of clients to make ends meet.

- Despite best intentions, you'll end up unable to deliver the client service and constant communication that you could if you did less volume.

- You will not get to know your clients as well and you cannot do much hand-holding.

- You get to serve a large amount of people.

- You help people who are lower-income be able to have access to excellent legal services.

As Neiman Marcus or even something in the middle like Macy's:

- You make a livable profit through the pricing you set for your cases.

- You're able to tailor your law firm for the efficiencies needed to deliver client service and maintain communications at the levels you prefer.

    o Extremely fast turnaround times

    o Regular and constant communications

    o Every single phone call returned

- You get to know your clients well.

- You can provide the one-on-one attention and hand-holding that your clients want.

Many solo practitioners are accidental Walmarts. They believe that slashing prices is the only way to get new business, and so they inadvertently have to sacrifice customer service for a volume practice.

It turns out that clients, or my clients at least, really want that high-level experience. They want a monthly phone call, email, and text message just to let them know that there is nothing new going on the case. They are willing to pay a premium for it.

We judge other lawyers for charging more. In turn, it makes us charge less. But if you think about it, Walmart doesn't care what Neiman Marcus is doing, and Neiman Marcus doesn't care what Walmart is doing. They have different models and totally different goals. One is not better than the other. They're just different.

What do you want your firm to be?

What do you want the experience with your firm to be like? What kind of experience do you want your clients to have? What do you want their interactions with your firm to be like? What types of cases do you want to handle? How do you want to be known?

Give this some serious thought, and then you can begin to build your firm around it. Not just with fees, but the entire firm experience—from the way everyone dresses, to the way clients are addressed, to client communication, to the client experience, and beyond.

<u>Workbook</u>

Now it's your turn! Go to page 10 of the Workbook and fill out the exercises for Chapter 1. Visit: http://bit.ly/LFBS-Book

Chapter Four: Sales

You are a saleswoman (or man). Yes, you are. And sales isn't dirty or slimey or sleazy. Sales is all about getting business. Sales is one of the most under-discussed topics when people talk about how to grow and run a law firm, which makes it one of the skills that is most severely lacking in law firms. Sales will allow you to grow and you need to understand sales in order to have more success in your business.

People don't walk over price

Let's start the Sales chapter with an important point: People do not walk away over price.

Our entire industry sets fees completely wrong. We set them based on what we think clients will pay or on what others charge or on the wages that people earn and the particular circumstances of our particular clients.

We think that if we get the price wrong, we will not get business. But this is completely incorrect.

The reason people don't hire has almost nothing to do with price.

When someone comes in to see an attorney, they need to understand:

1. That they need legal services

2. That they need it now

3. That they need it from you

If you do not do help them see these three things, they will walk.

Whether your price is $1,500 or $15,000 makes no difference. If you can't show them that they need legal services from you right now, they are gone.

Take a hard look at the way that you are communicating with clients and potential clients about fees.

The price needs to be the last of your worries. Focus on making sure you hit the 3 points above.

- Tell them they need legal services.

Simply tell them, "Yes, I can solve your problem. I can do X for you."

- Explain why they need your services now.

Show them the urgency of the situation. What will happen if they don't get your legal services now? Why do they need it now?

I say something like, "You qualify for the T Visa. I need you to know that it is urgent that you take action in your case, because people with DUI's are being arrested, detained, and held without bond. That means that even with a lawyer, you will be forced to stay in jail for a long time. But if we apply for this T visa now, there's a chance that it could protect you in case immigration ever came looking for you."

I created urgency and then I showed the solution to the problem.

- Show them they need to get the legal service from you.

In a nutshell, tell the client why you are the best attorney for the case.

Here's something I say:

"I can get this case filed for you in one week. If you go to any other lawyers, I can guarantee that they don't work as fast as we do and are not as organized as us. You need legal protection right away. You can't afford to wait.

If you work with us, within a week you will have your case filed, and hopefully it will provide you some protection. Plus, you officially have me as your lawyer in case anything comes up in the meantime."

That's it. Two paragraphs of information, short and to the point.

Now, the price.

There's no need to dread the part where you ask for the pricet. After following the above three points, your client should already be sold. It shouldn't matter what number comes out of your mouth. He should understand, very clearly, why it is that he needs to hire you right now.

$10,000? Fine. He'll find a way to get you the money.

It's not slimy or sleazy *as long as it is true*. In the case I mentioned, the urgency is 100% fact. Find the urgency in your own cases and the protection you can offer your clients. Sometimes you don't realize what is urgent because it's such common knowledge for you. For example, I used to always forget to tell my clients with DUI's what I mentioned above because for me it is something that is very commonplace for me and something I know very well. However, whatever urgent situation that applies to your cases, your clients might not know about at all. It is imperative that you inform them.

Value-Based Quoting™

Getting paid is an exchange of value. You are bringing value to the client by bettering his life with your legal services and solving a difficult issue in his life. The client brings you value by paying you money.

It is a value exchange.

You provide life-changing services to your clients. No matter what area you practice in, you are providing legal services that will impact the lives of your clients somehow.

Value-based quoting helps you communicate the value that you bring to your clients.

Usually when we quote a client, we tell them what they qualify for, and we tell them what the price is, and then we over-explain all of the legal steps we'll take. What's missing is the value we'll bring to the client.

The client needs to understand the life-changing service that you are providing.

Instead of going through painstaking detail about the legal process and what legal steps you are going to take, focus instead on the benefits to your clients. Here is what I say to my clients:

"The goal here is to get you a work permit in the United States, and then, in a few years, your green card. You have been here for a long time, and you have been working very hard to establish yourself and support your family. By having the T Visa, you will be here legally. You will be able to work legally. You will finally be able to live here safely without the fear of being deported."

They don't need to know *how* you are going to get them the legal benefit, rather they need to know only how that benefit will change their lives. Tell them the value of your services.

When you explain your value, you need to explain it in terms of the benefits your client will receive through the legal process and through working with you.

Do this before you talk about the price. This makes the client excited and even impatient to get started!

Value first, then the price. Communicating the value you bring gives you confidence about the price.

Once you get to quoing your price, don't end with the price! Many lawyers just go through the consult and end with the price, which is a big mistake.

After you give the price and ask for any questions the client may have, you next move on to tell the client what you need from him to get started on the case, such as documents and information. Ideally you have this written down in a list that you can provide in the consultation.

Then you conclude with how to get started with your representation. This is so common-sense that most of us tend to overlook it. You need to tell the client explicitly, "In order to get started on the case, _____." Tell the client what the next steps are on how to hire you, such as call to schedule the sign up appointment, email back the signed contract, etc.

Value-based quoting at a glance

Step 1. Communicate the value and benefits the client will get through the legal services you will provide. This is the longest part of your consultation.

Step 2. Give the price.

Step 3. Give a list of the information and documents needed.

Step 4. Tell the client how to get started with your representation.

As you can see, value-based quoting focuses on the value, not the quote. Give it a try! Practice your client-benefit-focused script. Always think of your consultation as a sales presentation.

The Consultation is a Sales Presentation

As I mentioned in the previous chapter on paid consults, the consultation is key for profitability. If you don't have consultations, you don't get new business. If you don't convert consultations into paying clients, then you don't have a firm. That's why the consultation is arguably the most important process in your legal business.

And that's why we need to do every consultation right. Instead of over-explaining like we were taught, we should make the consultation all about the client.

It's All About Them

Your consultation is a sales presentation. Plain and simple. If you have ever gone to any sales presentation in your life, you know that the best ones are the ones that "sell" you on what the benefit of the product or service is to you.

Think back on the car or property sales presentations you've seen. They all have one thing in common: you. Your experience. The benefits to your life. You upleveling in some sort of way.

That is how your consultation needs to be. It needs to be all about the client. In the Ally Lozano Sales Academy, we go deeper into this.

The 4 questions your potential client needs answered in a consultation:

1. Can you help me?

2. How long will it take?

3. How much will it cost?

4. What do you need from me?

Notice that they are not asking you to break down, step-by-step, how it is you are going to help them. **They just need to know you *can* help them.**

Many lawyers understandably hesitate over this question, because sometimes the outcome is impossible to predict and they can't guarantee they'll win the case.

Still, your consultation can focus on the following:

- The client wants to know if they can apply for something, if they are eligible for something, if you can give them the protection that they need, and if you can do it soon. This requires a simple yes or no- they are either eligible or they are not.

- If you are not 100% sure of the outcome, tell them that, but do not dwell on it and over-explain. Assure your clients that you have a backup plan if things do not turn out hte way that they had hoped.

    o In the *simplest* way possible. You can say, "We can apply for X, and if we win, we win Y. But if we lose, then Z will happen. And I have a plan for what we can do if that happens." That's pretty much all that needs to be said about it.

    o For the love of all that is holy, please do not go down every single possible contingency and all of the possible outcomes of each contingency. There is no need for this. It isn't our 1L year posing hypos. This is a real life scenario that has a likely outcome (or 2 or 3), and a backup plan for each one. That's all that your clients need to know.

The uncertainty of outcomes is one of the reasons that we over-explain in consults. We feel like we want the client to be fully informed of every possible outcome, every single hypothetical possibility, because we want them to fully understand every risk.

Our over-explaining comes from a good place. But it's just confusing for the client.

Regardless of how educated or uneducated a client is, keep your consultations simple and focus on the client benefits. Leave the "hows" to yourself to work on after you are hired.

The Sales Presentation

One of the most important elements of the sales presentation is printed materials for clients to take home with them. You want everyone to leave your office with written information.

Make sure everything is branded to reinforce your brand and your name recognition. The documents you give will also provide your clients with great reference materials.

The best way to do the sales presentation is with a branded folder that contains printed materials for clients. The things you should include are:

- Infographic with an overview of the legal process

    - A checklist, flowchart, or map of the most important steps in the case from beginning to end

    - You can tell them easily where you are in the case, what's left to do, etc.

- Quote sheet with the price of the case

    - The price of your services

    - A list of what the price includes and a list of what the price does not include (with an estimate of how much each additional item costs)

    - Payment options: full payment price, payment plans/credit card options

- Document list of the required documents and information

    - Don't worry about what the client will or won't do with your document list (i.e. take the list and try to do the case himself). The client is paying for your consultation and your information. Try to see it that way instead of fearing that the client will take your list and run.

    - Focus on the value they get (the document list is part of the value exchange of the consultation) and the efficiency that it will bring to your firm (if they engage you, you can get their cases out the door quickly because you'll have everything you need).

    - See this as just another perk of doing *paid* consults with you.

- Steps on how to begin the case with you

    - Can be included in the document sheet or the quote sheet.

"In order to get started..."

- Call our office to schedule a sign-up appointment

- The sign-up appointment will be scheduled for approximately 2 hours

- For the sign-up appointment, you need to bring your payment

- Though it is not required to have all of the documents in your case, when you come in to sign up, it is best to bring as many as you can so that we can work quickly on your case

Presentation Folder

You can give all of the above documents in a presentation folder. Brand it. It doesn't have to be expensive. You can buy a folder and stick on a mailing label with your information if you don't want the expense of printing fully-branded folders. That's how I did it for years.

I get my folders in different colors so I can have presentation folders ready by case type. By this I mean that one of my case types is prepared in the blue folder, another is prepared in a black folder, and so on. For my 3 main case types, I have 50 quote folders prepped. When I am in a consult and the client qualifies for something, I grab a folder and use it as a guide during the consult.

Here's what typically happens:

- I walk them through the infographic.

- When I finish, I ask if they have questions and 9 times out of 10, it's, "How much does it cost?"

- I flow to the next page in the folder, the quote sheet. I ask again if they have any questions. And usually, it's, "What documents do I need?"

- I ease right into the document list and then explain how to get started on the case.

Once you find this groove, you will love it! It will transform your consults to serve your clients better, *and* it will have the added benefit of making you more money.

Your Unique Advantage

Competition is a myth. You are not in competition with anyone. There is no one who does what you do the way you do it.

What is key in sales and marketing is knowing—and expressing to your clients—what makes you different from everyone else. Every single person who works for you needs to know this and be able to tell it to clients and potential clients.

Here's an exercise: Ask your team (including you) to list the five reasons why people should hire you and your firm. Have them send their lists to you directly so no one is influenced by anyone else's answers. This will hopefully guide you to understanding your unique advantage.

Expressing your unique advantage to clients

We feel like we're bragging if we say something good about ourselves. But no one will know that we do great work unless we tell them.

What do clients want to know?

- Have you handled a case like theirs before?

    o   If you specialize in this, if you are an expert in this, tell them that! They'll feel good about hiring you.

- Are you the right lawyer for your client?

    o   Of course! Don't feel bad about saying this. It's not putting other lawyers down. You're not be the right lawyer for every client—that's just not realistic—but you happen to be the right lawyer for a specific client. Say so.

You have special experience, skills, interests, and life stories that make you different from everyone else. No one can compete with you. No one. And you can't compete with anyone else. You are you. And there's nothing better than that!

In your branded folder, you can include a one-page handout with bullet points about what makes you and your firm different. It will help set expectations with your firm as well as guide people to understand why you're the right lawyer for them.

Create a Salesforce In Your Firm

You and your staff need to be sales masters. Your team is your front line. They handle your phones. They meet with your clients. They need to be ready for all of the same things that you are when it comes to sales.

This means you have to train them! The best way to do that is with scripts.

Scripts don't need to be robotic or read word for word. They're a general guide to what needs to be said.

Here is a sample phone script:

- [Greeting] my name is _____, how can I help you?

  - Greeting ideas:

    - Good morning/ Good afternoon

    - Thank you for calling [law firm name]

- The person will say why they are calling. Then ask for their name, and *remember it*.

  - Tip: Write it down if you need to.

  - Do not ask for the person's name more than once! Get it from the beginning

- Be sure to use the person's name at least three times in the interaction

If first time caller:

- Remember that they likely have never worked with a lawyer before so you need to honor that, and understand that they may not understand that they have to pay for a consultation.

- Talk about the benefits of the consultation before stating the price.

- "The way that it works here is that we schedule you for a consultation to come meet with the lawyer so you can tell her about your legal case. It is scheduled for one hour, and you can explain your situation, and ask her all of the questions that you have. She will put together a plan for what you can do and how much it will cost. The consultation is in-person in our office in [city], and is $150. We require payment at the time of scheduling the appointment. Is there a day of the week that works best for you?"

- At this point, you will know if they are willing to pay or not.

- Let them pick the time and date *before* taking their payment.

- Use positive, encouraging words.

- Schedule the appointment, and take the payment.

- If they have the appointment all set but then say they don't have a card, ask when you can call them back to set up their payment. Put this information in the follow-up system.

- If they schedule and make the payment:

    - "Thank you for making the payment. We look forward to seeing you on [time and date] at our office. I am going to send you a text message with the appointment information and our address to confirm. If you need anything in the meantime, please feel free to call, text, or email."

- Sign off with something such as, "have a great day," or "thank you for the call," or "I will see you soon."

If current client:

- Pull up their case in the case management system so you can see the notes about the most recent activity in the case.

- If they ask to speak with the lawyer say, "Sure thing. But is there anything that I can answer for you?"

- The majority of the time the question will be, "I just want to know what's going on in my case."

- Use the notes to give them the most relevant update. "I am looking at your file right now, and I see that [details of recent activity]."

- If the person still insists on talking with the lawyer, find out if there is anything that you can ask the lawyer on the client's behalf

    - "Are there any questions I can pass along to her?"

- If the person says, "No, I just want to talk to the lawyer," then schedule them for a 15-minute phone meeting.

- Explain that the phone meeting is a formal meeting with the lawyer. You can find your best wording for this, but here is an idea:

    - "Sure thing. I am going to schedule you for a formal phone meeting with the lawyer. This will ensure that you get all of your questions answered, and she will be prepared to have a conference about your case. I can pass on any questions in advance if you would like."

- Before hanging up, be sure to always say, "If you need anything else, feel free to call, email, or text!"

    - We want them to feel like we are always there for them.

    - We want them to know that they are always welcome and not a bother!

Another part of the script is when clients call with comments or complaints.

Overcoming Specific Comments/ Objections of Clients

Your staff should be prepared to handle specific comments and objections from clients and potential clients. Your staff should respond with the highest level of customer service and with an eye on sales.

Here are the main objections that we hear:

- A client states that s/he doesn't understand why s/he needs to pay for the consult

- A client complains about the price of a case

- A client says, "All you do is call to ask for money. You don't ever call about my case. But you do call about money."

- A client says that we haven't done anything in the case

Let's take these one-by-one:

Paying for the Consult

Remember that no one walks over price. This is an opportunity for your team to show them why they need this consultation now and why they need it from your firm.

See how your staff currently answers this. They may already have great ways to handle the objection, or there may be room for improvement.

If the client is saying that other lawyers don't charge for consultations, some responses you and your staff can offer are:

- "The lawyer here is one of the best lawyers in the state. She is extremely well-known because of the great results that she gets for her clients. I don't know about the other lawyers, but I know that it will be well worth it for you to come and speak to her."

- "The lawyer here is excellent, and people are always lining up to get an appointment with her. [Include some of your qualifications: She speaks Spanish. She is dedicated to the Latino community, and works almost exclusively with Mexicans, so she will understand your case better than any other lawyer around.]"

    - Note that this is about me specifically, but I included it to give you an idea of how your staff can use your uniqueness to "sell" the consult here.

Don't be shy. It's not bragging to tell clients you are an excellent lawyer. They won't know unless you tell them!

Complaining About the Price of a Case

The best way to handle this objection is to agree. They need to feel acknowledged for what they are investing in this. Whether it is $500 or $5,000 or $15,000, it is a lot of money to a client. So we need to honor that.

Examples:

- "Yes, it is a lot of money. And if we win this case, it will change your life and the life of your family."

- "Yes, it definitely is an investment."

- "You're right. It is a lot of money, and our goal is to make sure that every penny that you spend is well worth in terms of results."

If you take the Ally Lozano Sales Academy, you will be armed and ready to overcome these objections. But your staff may not be. You need to help them be able to say these same things and express your unique advantage.

Acknowledge the money output, *and then state the value.* Everything always comes back to the value you bring to your clients.

Your staff likely feels uncomfortable when clients complain about money, so help them know how to handle it better.

<u>Client Says You Only Call About Money and Not About Their Case</u>

This can be very frustrating and overwhelming because the client feels mad and you and your team immediately feel on the defensive. Again, any time that the client is expressing anger or frustration is a great time for excellent customer service and sales.

Here are some ideas for responses:

- "I understand it feels frustrating to you that we are calling for a payment, and it feels like you have not had an update on your case. Would you like to talk about the latest details of your case?"

- Kindly refer to the last time you spoke. "Well today I am calling because we have to take the next step in your case, which requires the next payment. As we discussed two weeks ago, [summary of what you discussed], and now it's time to take the next step forward."

- If it's your staff, they can say something like, "We do need to take the payment on the case, however, after I take the payment I can set you up with a phone meeting with the lawyer."

Don't start a back and forth with your client with a defensive response like, "That's ridiculous! I just talked to you last week!"

Don't argue. Sometimes a client just needs to vent. Let them. You and your team can find a positive way to move forward.

<u>Client Says You Haven't Done Anything in Their Case</u>

It's a fear-based statement. Your client is nervous about their case and worried it's not progressing. They're scared. That's it.

That being said, when clients tell me that I haven't done anything in their cases, it gets me. Every. Single. Time. If you want to bait me, tell me that I haven't done anything in your case. BUT, this is the same as everything else we have been talking about here. It's another great opportunity for customer service. I know it's hard, but don't take it personally.

Show your clients that you are working for them. Here are some sample responses:

- "We are working very hard on your case."

- "Your case is important to us."

- "You are very important to me and my firm."

- "Your case matters to us."

- "We are working hard for you."

They might reply. "Well, it doesn't feel like it," or, "I never hear from you."

Address that. "I understand that you would like more contact from me. I will work hard to be in regular contact with you. How about we schedule a call for next month to check in?"

This will satisfy them and take away the negative charge on the next contact. It's one small thing that can make a big difference!

With these responses, you and your staff can really become masters at sales.

5 Tips to Become a Master Saleswoman (or man)

Now that you are rocking your consultations as sales presentations, expressing your uniqueness to clients, and embracing your value, it's time to take it up a notch. I want you to be the best saleswoman (or man) that you can possibly be.

Here are 5 tips that will help you become a master saleswoman:

1. Always agree with the client

The client is right, even when he is wrong. There is no need to point out everything that is wrong and correct it. Lawyers are literal people. Arguing is in our blood. But there is no need for that with our clients. If you must disagree, do so gracefully.

For example, if they want to explain to you how the law works (as if you didn't already know!), you can say, "Wow, you've really done a great job with trying to be as informed about the process as possible. That gives us a great starting point! Let me recap the process to make sure we are on the same page."

In that example, you have given them a compliment. You have acknowledged how hard they have worked to become informed. You have shown them appreciation. Yes, maybe they are completely wrong, but by acknowledging them in a positive way, you can move forward and give them the most relevant, important information.

This will affirm your client's decision to hire you.

2. Customer service remains at the forefront

Every single interaction in your law firm needs to have your customers in mind.

- How do they want to feel?

- How do they want to be treated?

- How do they want to be communicated with?

- What kind of feeling do you want them to have while they are in the office?

Making the client feel relaxed and respected is the key to building trust and building the important relationship between a client and his attorney.

In our firm, we call it honoring the client experience. We honor the fact that they have made the difficult decision to move forward with a case with us. We honor the fact that they are going through a difficult time when they reach out to us and want to hire us. We honor the investment that they make into our firm.

Customer service is a non-negotiable in a law firm. It is the basis of all sales.

3. Constantly Improve your Communication

Always focus on how you can communicate better.

- Video tape yourself giving a consultation—with the client's permission—so you can review how you do.

- Or do a fake consultation so you can review it and rate your performance.

- Do consultations with your family, friends, or staff. Do your pitch, and quote them. Ask for feedback.

    o Did you over-explain?

    o Was anything unclear?

    o Where can you improve?

Focus on the benefits to the client in the simplest way possible. Find a way to explain complex matters in non-complex terms, with visual aids if possible.

4. Treat Objections as Complaints

People love to complain. People complain about the weather all of the time and they aren't asking for anyone to do anything about it- they just want others to know how they feel about it. The same goes with clients.

When clients say, "Wow that's a lot of money," or "Don't you offer a discount?" we start to feel stressed and pressured.

We treat this as if they are *objecting* to the price, and we think we should lower it or they'll walk away.

But they're not objecting, they're just complaining. And we need to acknowledge that complaint. They want you to understand that it is a lot of money for them. They are investing in your services. They want you to recognize that they are putting their lives and problems into your hands, which is scary for them.

All of it can be solved by saying, "Yes, it is a lot of money." Or "I understand."

"I understand" is a powerful phrase. You can add to it something like, "This is an investment into your future. I will do my best for you." Anything to reassure them.

Reassurance is ultimately what they want and need.

5. Be fearless when quoting your fee

Always give your price confidently. Remember the value you bring to your clients' lives. Get rid of the fear and the incorrect thinking that one client can make or break your firm.

Clients don't usually walk over price. Tap in to all of your sales skills to help close the deal. If a client does walk away because of the price, let them. It will not break you. Do you hear me? IT WILL NOT BREAK YOU!

Remember the great work that you do, and always quote your fee like the excellent lawyer that you are.

Workbook

Now it's your turn! Go to page 12 of the Workbook and fill out the exercises for Chapter 1. Visit: http://bit.ly/LFBS-Book

Chapter 5: Management

As the CEO of your law firm, you need to have a good grasp of management in your firm. Even starting out as a solo, you'll have staff. Good management is a big part of growth and success, because this is how you hire *and retain* the best people.

When to Hire

In my experience, you know it's time to hire when you keep asking yourself, "Should I hire someone else?"

Here are three other important questions to help you consider whether it is time to hire someone new:

- **Are you spending your day doing a lot of things someone else could be doing?**

    - Are you answering phones? Making copies? Inputting data? Processing mail? The best thing that you can do with your time is practice law since that's the skill that you have that is not easily replaced by someone else, so try to move toward that.

As you grow, you can use this same test to figure out if and when you need another lawyer. For example, if you are spending a lot of time in short, initial court hearings and your time could be better spent in consultations or meeting with clients, then it may be a good time to bring in a contract attorney or consider hiring an associate.

If your time is better spent being the rainmaker—and currently your time is being spent in court—then it's something that's important to be aware of so you can start considering whether you need to bring someone new in.

- **Is everyone on your team maxing out at 100%?**

    - If you ask your staff if they need additional help or if they are maxing out on their caseloads, they will almost always say yes. However, if you look at their time and how they are using it, they might not be maxing out at 100%.

- Make sure that everyone is truly at 100% capacity. If you have three people on your staff who are operating at 80%, bringing them up to 100% might solve the gap without needing to hire another person.

One way to do this is to try to avoid chitchat and questions in person. Use chat platforms (Slack, G-chat, etc) for urgent matters, your case management system for case-related matters, and sticky notes on filings to ask questions, make edits, etc. in order to enable you and your staff to communicate far more efficiently than regularly interrupting each other.

At first, cutting out in-person interactions might seem cold and distant, but everyone loves it in my firm. We all want to be productive and send our cases out the door as soon as possible. We have been able to maximize our team and run lean because of it.

Ensuring productivity and efficiency means you don't overhire.

- **Where do you need help the most?**

Our default mode is to hire more legal assistants. It's usually all hands on deck for the cases, but you probably sorely need help in bookkeeping, billing, marketing, and so on. It is a big mistake to have legal assistants do legal work plus these other essential tasks in your law firm.

When you grow, you need staff who are experts in their assigned tasks. They become experts if they *have* assigned tasks instead of multitasking as the need arises.

- If you don't have one yet, you might need a legal assistant who helps you on cases.

- You might need an admin or a business manager. Someone who takes care of the business instead of cases.

- Ask your staff to provide bullet points of their tasks. This would show you who's doing what, what you still need done, what you can streamline, and whether you're maxing out your staff and need to hire.

Asking those three questions is the start. Always focus on efficiency for your team. This includes hiring *and* thinking through your processes.

You can really lower turnover and maximize your team by thinking through each one of the above questions and working to streamline your firm at every step—including how to hire.

How to Hire

Hiring is one of the hardest parts of management. If you haven't yet, I highly recommend that you read the book, *Who* by Geoff Smart and Randy Street. It is incredibly helpful to help you figure out how to hire and not fall into what the author calls, "voodoo hiring practices."

Let's start with some "how to hire" basics:

Job Description

Based on what you lack and what you need done in your law firm, write the job description.

For example, you may think you need a legal assistant (it's hardwired for us!) but if your needs are actually in billing, mailing, and other in-office/client communications, you need a customer service specialist or admin.

Where to Advertise the Job

Even when you are not actively hiring, always be looking for your next hire.

Whenever you meet someone who could be a good fit for your firm, give them your card and tell them that if they ever are interested in a job, they can contact you.

- Use your network. Let people know about a job opening specifically, but also ask them to let you know about good talent that they come across.

- Many experts recommend paying people a "finder's fee" to someone who finds you a good hire.

- Other major places: Indeed, Monster, Upwork, etc.

    o It can be worth it to pay a small amount to increase the visibility of the job listing and access to applicants with high levels of talent.

How to Quickly Narrow the Applicant Pool

Look for attention to detail

- Ask them why they want to work for you and your firm.

    o If they do not follow this instruction, you weed out those who sent out résumés en masse without knowing what job they are applying for.

Look for the ability to follow instructions

- Provide specific instructions and discard applicants who can't follow them. For example, ask them to do one of the following:

    o Include a code word *at the end* of their cover letter.

    o List three references but with emails instead of phone numbers.

    o Use a specific subject line in their application email

There were times I let applicants who didn't follow instructions slide because their experience and skills met what I needed. Without fail, when I asked them why they wanted to work for me, they would say they didn't know.

Before moving forward with the next steps in the hiring process, remember that you owe it to your firm and to your clients to find the best possible person for the job. Be selective.

Phone Interview

Doing in-person interviews with people is extremely time consuming, and a 15-minute phone interview can reveal a lot.

Some of the questions that I like to ask are:

- What interests you about working for our firm?

- Tell me about your current position.

- What are the top skills from your current position that could be applicable in our firm?

Email Assignment

If everything has gone well with the phone interview, then follow up with an email assignment. It shouldn't be something too time-intensive, but it should test their attention to detail and resourcefulness.

If you give them a form to fill out, do they send it back to you with typos? (I experienced this!)

You can assume that the work quality that they send back is their absolute best given that they want the position. So if the work has errors when they're supposedly at their best, imagine a regular day at the office.

What I like about email assignments is that they take my feelings out of the equation. I am terrible at in-person meetings, because I give people the benefit of the doubt—especially if someone is likeable. Written activities take my emotions out of it and shine a light on the work.

In-Person Interview

When a candidate makes it through the screening steps above, focus on the job, on what you need, during the in-person interview. Don't get distracted by personality and commonalities. Those are great. But you need the role filled for the tasks you need done, not the likability of the person.

I really recommend that you get the book *Who* and follow their questions to the letter. In addition, I like to ask the following:

- What are three skills and abilities that you will bring to this position that help you excel?

- What makes you the best person for the position?

- What are three things that you want to accomplish within the next five years?

References

CALL REFERENCES EVERY SINGLE TIME! A colleague was ready to hire someone, but then called the reference of the lawyer. The previous employer said, "F- no. Do not hire this person." And here she thought that she had found the best fit for her firm and almost didn't call references!

I have had this situation, too. I thought the person was so great and I was so excited that I even hugged her. I was so smitten with the hire that I did not call references. She goes down in the history of my businesses as the worst hire I have ever made. It was a disaster.

You may think that you don't need to hear the nice things the references would say after you *connect* with a good candidate. But that's not always the case. In fact, it's pretty much never the case.

Also, do not limit yourself to the references that they list. Ask them who they reported to in their previous positions and call those people too. It's a good idea to even call and talk to their subordinates to get a feel as to how they treated people who had a lower rank than them. Do your research and homework to make sure you find the right hire.

Attract the Best Talents With Better Benefits

The best talent wants benefits. If you have the benefits, you get the talent. If you don't, you won't.

The expenses are much smaller than you think. Provide health benefits, paid time off and sick time, short term disability insurance, and a Simple IRA for retirement. It is worth investing in these to attract and keep the best people.

Hopefully these tips will help you make the right hire(s) for your firm. And when you get them, managing them properly helps you keep them.

What You Need to Manage People

Once you have your dream team in place, the following helps you be a smart manager. As CEO of your law firm, you are the manager of all your employees.

- Policy Manual

- Training Manual

- Employee File

- Payroll Processor

Policy Manual

A policy manual is *key* if you have even one employee. You need to have your policies and procedures written down and in place.

Writing your policy manual can be a beast of a task. We have one already done for Law Firm Business School students!

As a primer, here's what you need to include:

- **Dress code**

    o   Think of the culture in your firm and your clients. What do your clients want to see? Adapt to that, whether it's business professional or business casual.

    o   Have a visual template. Lay out rules of about tattoos, if any.

    o   If you have casual Fridays, define what is and isn't allowed.

    o   Your standards should be clear.

- **Computer and electronics usage**

    o   People are attached to their phones. You may want a strict policy of lunch and break times only for phone access: turned off or silenced and in drawers at all other times. If someone has a situation where they need to be contactable via phone, they can talk about it with you/your business manager.

    o   Office hours are for working. We try to get a ton done in 40 hours, and we can't have distractions such as the phone.

    o   Have clear policies on TV and computer use. This is the age of Netflix and you need to decide if people streaming shows and movies is something that is acceptable in your office.

- **Attendance Policies**

    o   Working Hours: Determine what time people should start working. It should be clear that you mean working and not getting started with their coffee and morning chit-chat.

    o   Breaks: How long? How often?

- PTO and sick time: How is it earned? How can it be accessed? What is the process for obtaining PTO and sick time?

- Pay period: When and how people are paid?

- Paid holidays: You might not be off for every federal holiday, but which ones do you have? Any other breaks like winter break, too?

- **Discipline Policies**

  - Minor and major offenses, and their consequences, should be outlined.

  - Your policy manual contains the rules—and the consequences for rule-breaking.

Training Manual

A training manual is essential to ensuring that your firm is systems-dependent and not people-dependent. Both the policy manual and the training manual need to serve as the keepers of information—otherwise the keeper of information is you, and you will constantly be interrupted. You also will always have to be the trainer of anyone new.

Anyone who comes into your firm, at any time, can be asked to do something and should be able to figure out how to do it by looking at the training manual.

- If you get this right, you don't have to train people at all.

- In case time is tight and you hired in a crunch, or life happens and you have to jump into crisis mode, the training manual can get people pretty much through the main things they have to do.

That's the goal.

If you have only one person on staff, or even if you have no staff at all, you should be creating your training manual. It's a living, breathing document.

Creating a training manual can be easy.

- Have everyone, including yourself, outline what you/ they do in the firm. Have them provide you with a bullet-pointed list as the outline.

- Once you have outlines of every single task done in your office, you and your team can go through and write step-by-step guides on how to do the tasks each of you do.

- Set deadlines for completion, and have annual reviews to make sure the training manual still works.

You can refer back to the manual when trying to figure out how to hire and the exact role(s) you need to fill.

Employee Files

There should be three files for every employee in your office:

1. I-9 File

2. Employee General File

3. Employee Medical File

I know that when we think of files, we think of hard files, but the easiest way to keep these files is to store them electronically. They should be stored in a place where other employees do not have access to them given that they have sensitive information, such as social security numbers and medical information.

Let's take these one by one.

1. I-9 File

The I-9 file. This should be one file in which all employee's I-9s are stored.

- The I-9 ensures all your employees can legally work in the U.S.

   o There is a list of documents required to be used to document legal authorization to work, and it is recommended that you maintain a copy of those documents along with the I-9 forms in the event that there is a workplace audit.

It is very easy to manage the I-9s using various different payroll services. I use and love Gusto—they allow people to input their own information and electronically store the I-9s through their system. You just have to verify it. It is a very easy system, and it makes the files much easier to manage.

2.   Employee General File

This is a file for your personal reference about an employee. Some important documents to include are:

- Signed Confidentiality Agreement

- Signed confirmation of receipt and review of policy manual

- Signed confirmation of receipt and review of training manual

- Non-disclosure agreement and non-compete agreement, where appropriate

- Employee reviews

- Raise information

- Disciplinary actions

Optional inclusions:

- Employee résumé and reference information

- Reference letters

3. Employee Medical File

These must be kept separate from the other files and kept very secure because of their sensitive information. This file should include doctors notes, disability information, and any and all other medical information about an employee, including any special needs for medical insurance and the like.

Payroll Processor

Paper checks are things of the past. Make sure you can get everyone going with direct deposit.

There are a lot of things that you have to do when you hire people and process payroll, like file certain reports with the state, complete quarterly reports, pay taxes each payroll, and more. It can feel overwhelming.

That's why you need an easy-to-use payroll processor. I use and love Gusto. It makes everything extremely easy for my team and me. They even manage our health insurance.

However, there are a lot of other companies make it increasingly easy to manage payroll. Your bank may even be affiliated with a payroll processor. Choose one and get payroll taken care of. You have so many other management tasks on your list so this one should be easy to check off.

Creating Values/ Pillars of Your Law Firm

You became a lawyer because you stand for something. You have a passion for a cause or issue. You love what you do. You wouldn't have made it through the bar exam if you didn't think that you were going to have a career that you loved.

You started a law firm out of that passion. You wanted to be able to do you work and needed a way to be able to do it.

Out of your passion and belief system, you need to articulate the principles you want to guide your law firm. Here are mine to help get you thinking about yours so you can put them into words:

1. Overcommuncation with clients

2. Extreme efficiency (fast turnarounds)

3. Excellent customer service

4. Great results

5. Creative legal solutions

As we run our own businesses, we are often caught up thinking about just one thing... price. We worry about anything related to price ("If I charge too much, I won't get business." "If I charge too much other lawyers will judge me." "If my prices are too high, it means I don't care enough.") This makes our values and pillars inadvertently focus on pricing and nothing else. We get caught up thinking about pricing and we forget to enumerate other things that are important to us and our law firm as a business.

This is why it is important to identify and state your firm's values. Your pillars and values should be written down, so you can ensure that you're living up to them and enabling your firm to live up to them.

For example, if you value having the lowest price, then by all means add it to your list of values. But know that if another one of your values is client hand-holding throughout the process, then it is going to be difficult, if not impossible, to give your clients that experience and have the lowest prices at the same time. That is why it is important to give your values serious thought and consideration.

Once you define your values, reconcile them with your law firm. That means that you may have to let go of charging too little on cases so that you can maximize the experience that you offer clients, or you have to up the ante when it comes to client communication.

This reconciliation starts with you. How can you live up to your values better?

Where have you failed or fallen short, and how can you change and improve?

Leadership starts at the top, and we have to work on ourselves before we are able to bring this to our firms. We have to be the example.

From there, how can you help your team be better? What specific ways can they change and improve?

Once you get all of this together, distribute your values list to your team and hold a meeting to explain it to them.

I don't believe in micromanaging, so I depend on each person to use his or her best judgment throughout the day. My team uses our five values to guide the small decisions they have to make throughout the day.

By putting together the values your firm will stand for, you will inspire your team. Your values are pillars. They hold up your law firm and give you something to gauge every decision against within your firm. Your values make you unique and stand out from everyone else. And by living your values, you will find more enjoyment in your practice and firm.

Your Most Important Hire: A Business Manager

The business manager is the most important hire in your law firm. Usually lawyers talk about how they need more legal assistants and attorneys in their firms, but you almost never hear anyone talk about the need for a business manager.

If you have more than 50 cases in your law firm, you need a business manager. Lawyers hate the business operations, but these have to get done: payroll, managing staff, hiring, firing, sending client bills, receipts, handling difficult client situations, collecting money, and more. This is a full-time job.

If you don't have a full-time person doing these tasks, that means that you and your team are doing them, taking precious time and resources away from your cases and clients.

You can't do it all. Having one person in your firm who does not work on cases and instead works on your business is crucial.

Your business manager's responsibilities include:

- Payroll

- Pay bills

- Manage bank accounts

- Process payments

- Process receipts

- Prepare bills

- Manage client payment plans

- Manage firm benefits (such as healthcare, life insurance, disability insurance, etc)

- Pay quarterly taxes

- Manage business license renewals

- Manage time-off requests

- Recruit new employees

- Hire/Fire

- Ensure staff reviews are done

- Facilitate communication between attorney and staff

- Facilitate communication between attorney and clients

- Marketing management

- Manage business banking and contacts with the business banker

- Manage Bench.co

- Manage communications with CPA

- Manage credit card processing company

Now that's a list! And our business manager also occasionally does more. Like when we moved offices, he researched and toured places, negotiated the contract, met with designers to make sure the set up was correct, met with different internet and electricity providers to find the best rates and packages, scheduled and managed installation of those things, picked out the furniture, ordered the furniture, organized the move, and more.

There is no way that a lawyer with a full caseload can take all of that on.

The problem is that most of us try. I've worked at law firms that employed over 20 people in the past, and not one of them had a business manager.

Notice that there is something very important missing from the list of business manager tasks- case work. Many lawyers make the mistake that if someone is in the law firm working, then that person must work on case work. As lawyers we will always prioritize case work, which means that we will force everyone who does case work to make that their focus as well. Then the business management tasks will fall by the wayside and remain undone. When you bring in a business manager, his or her *only* job must be to manage the business.

Your business manager can do so much for you and your firm. You will have true *freedom* after delegating a lot of the tasks listed above. You will be able to do the work that you love, and allow your business to grow with a lot less intervention on your end.

Handling the Difficult Aspects of Management

No matter how great of a boss you are, even with a great team and a clearly defined policy manual, you'll face difficult people and situations that require disciplinary action.

This one of the most dreaded parts of handling staff, particularly if you're not good with confrontation.

Your policy manual is key to handling employee behavior.

- All terms of conduct you expect from your employees should be clear in the manual.

- It is extremely important that you don't let bad behavior slide. Small things can quickly become your employee's "normal."

- Behavior spreads. Anything your employees see you not enforcing become normalized *and adopted.*

Confrontation doesn't mean a throw-down, even though that's usually the first thing that we think when we hear that word.

It can be something as simple as a firm-wide email to remind your staff of the firm's policies. If someone was tardy, remind everyone about the time you should all start work.

That's the first step to help handle it, generally, without having to call anyone out specifically.

If you have staff who needs more direct correction, here are the next steps you can take:

Document Everything

Document every single interaction with staff about an issue.

If you discuss tardiness, lacking work quality, cell phone use, absences, etc, with an employee, always follow it up with an email so that there is documentation about the conversation.

The email should include:

- Summary of the issue discussed

- Summary of the discussion itself—your points and their points

- Plan of action to remedy the situation, and, when appropriate, the time frame in which you expect to see change

This email is not a formal write-up. It's a summary of understanding and a record. Save it to the employee's file.

Why document?

- It is important to have documentation in case this happens again in the future.

- Everyone's busy, you, your business manager, and even your employee will likely forget the details. An email keeps a record of what happened and what's been said.

- You'll have a reference in case another conversation is needed or if you have to escalate to a formal write-up.

Written Warning

A written warning is usually the first formal step of disciplinary action. The offense you discussed previously has been repeated, no improvement has been made.

- Have a meeting with the employee to discuss his/her problematic behavior.

- Mention the specific violations of the policy manual.

- Talk to the employee to understand their side and to find out if there have been any reasons for these certain behaviors.

- You both should have an opportunity to be heard.

- Discuss the changes you expect to see, the timeframe you expect to see them in, and the consequences if the behavior persists.

- Deliver the formal written warning. You and your employee both have a copy, and you both sign it to confirm issue and receipt.

- They can also formally respond to the warning in writing.

- Both the warning and the written response are saved in the employee's file

Temporary Suspension

Temporary Suspension is a disciplinary action that comes next if the employee doesn't comply with the written warnings. It could be a one-day, unpaid suspension, or more. Be sure that you comply with your state's employment laws. If you believe that this is the next right disciplinary step, it is always a good idea to consult an employment attorney.

Firing

No one likes firing, but some acts are egregious, and termination of employment is the action you need to take. Stealing, lying about something important, and behavior failures that violate what's in your policy *and* your company values are a few reasons that firing becomes necessary.

- Have a written statement about the termination and the reasons for it.

- When you call the person into your office to discuss the firing, it is best to have another person present as a witness.

- Get straight to the point. Tell them you are letting them go and the reasons why. Ask them to read over the document.

- They can ask any questions they may have.

- It's important to immediately collect the person's office keys, office/building access cards, and any other company property, as well as suspend his/her accounts such as email, access to your server, and more.

You might feel the above are harsh. I agree, taking disciplinary action is not fun or pleasant. But you have to think about your firm and your clients. Your clients deserve the best firm. Disruptive and destructive actions can negatively affect your other employees.

If you wait to take action, you will always end up regretting it.

Hiring, managing, and firing aren't for the faint of heart. Having a business manager helps.

You deserve the best business possible, and your employees deserve the best working environment. Everyone should buy into your mission, vision, and yes, your rules. Rules aren't there just for the sake of rules—they are there to serve the highest purpose of your work and your firm. That's why they're important.

Facing and taking action with difficult employees is one of the hardest parts of running a business, but it's worth it to make your firm grow.

Workbook

Now it's your turn! Go to page 14 of the Workbook and fill out the exercises for Chapter 1. Visit: http://bit.ly/LFBS-Book

Chapter 6: Marketing

Marketing is NOT a dirty word. There's a pervading belief that if you market your legal services, you are somehow "less" as a lawyer. Many believe that if you were truly a great lawyer, people would just find out about you, and you'd get business that way.

That is just bananas. You need clients to do great work *for*. You need to raise awareness of your name and your law firm's name in order to get people in the door.

This is why marketing is so important.

Even the U.S. Supreme Court recognized the importance of advertising and marketing for lawyers. When the state bar of Arizona tried to take away a lawyer's license for placing an advertisement, the case was appealed to the U.S. Supreme Court. The USSC determined that:

- More people could be served if lawyers advertised their cases, because a very large number of people were not getting access to the legal services they needed and didn't know how to find a lawyer.

- Lawyers would be unable to establish clientele if they weren't allowed to reach out to new clientele.

Bates v. State Bar of Arizona, 433 U.S. 350 (1977). You see how logical it is? Even the USSC says so!

Marketing is a conversation with your clients

It's not a dirty word. Marketing is simply a conversation with your potential clients, current clients, and past clients. Really, that's what it boils down to.

Everything that you write on your website and post on your social media is there to spark a conversation or to hold a conversation with your potential, current, and past clients.

When done right, everything that you put out there is a response to a question or pain point your ideal clients have. They want to know who can solve their problem.

You have to communicate that you are the lawyer who can solve that problem. That is what marketing is all about.

Defining Your Ideal Client

One of the biggest mistakes that lawyers make when trying to market their services is asking, "Where should I market" instead of asking the most important question, "To *whom* should I market?"

There are tons of ways to market—from online to billboards to print ads. But throwing out ads to try to get clients is not a way to have a successful marketing plan. If you want to get your marketing done, you don't just throw money at it and hope you got your message to the right people.

A marketing plan is easier and simpler than you think and it starts with your ideal client.

Your ideal client is the person you want to serve whose needs match your services.

For effective marketing, you have to figure out who that person is. **The beauty of defining your ideal client is you also create a practice that you absolutely love.**

Here are some questions to help you determine your Ideal Client:

- What cases do you love to do?

- If you could do just one case type every single day for the rest of your career, what would it be?

- Who are your favorite clients and what do they have in common?

- If you think about all of your clients in general, what commonalities stand out to you?

    - Are there more males or females?

    - What is the average age range?

    - What is the average education level?

    - Is there a specific job or jobs that the majority of your clients have?

It's really interesting when you start to think about who it is that you already serve. You might see similar legal issues, similar industries that people come from (i.e. tech industries, start ups, etc), similar family structures (i.e. blended families or LGBT families or unmarried couples with children), and more.

It is possible to have more than one Ideal Client. Some people have two (or more) completely distinct Ideal Clients. The first step is being able to define your Ideal Client/s, who they are, what they do, their pain points, and so on. Then you can figure out how to market to them. If there are two different Ideal Clients then you will need two separate and distinct marketing plans.

"Anyone who can pay" is NOT your Ideal Client. We want clients who can pay, of course, but that's not what you want to focus on when you're trying to market and grow the firm of your dreams.

For years, I worked on a case type with clients who could pay for my services. Unfortunately, those clients were also extremely high-maintenance and the work was unenjoyable. In the end, all the stress and my dissatisfaction with the work made it not worth it to me to continue bringing in those particular clients.

The main purpose of identifying your Ideal Client is to make your marketing dollars stretch. Having an Ideal Client doesn't mean you turn away cases. You have to make a living. If that means taking in cases that you don't enjoy but that pay the bills, so be it.

However with an Ideal Client in mind you can focus your marketing efforts toward attracting them. Time and money are your two most limited resources, so you want them to go as far as they can.

Spending $200 to try to get as many clients as you can is not an effective marketing strategy because it is not going to have a big impact in terms of getting people in the door for a consultation. Instead, spending $200 to try to reach the people who are the best fit for your firm is going to increase your return on that $200.

It will get more consultations, and not just that, it will attract people whose consultations *will* turn into new contracts. This means more money for you.

Talking to your Ideal Client makes them come in droves. With time, focusing on your ideal client creates a law firm you absolutely love. It's almost impossible to describe what it feels like to have a law firm with clients whose cases you enjoy doing every single day.

Compare that to the status quo of law firms who usually take on whatever cases come in the door. When I went solo, I continued that practice of "door law." I was jumping at the chance to have a new case. I constantly felt like I didn't have any money and I needed every single case I could competently handle.

Once I started focusing on my Ideal Clients through my marketing—my Facebook Live show, my Facebook for business page in general, my Avvo website, my firm website, and more—they started coming in droves. I fell in love with my practice again. I feel excited to come to work and to my cases.

I love the work that I do and the clients that I serve. Everyone in my firm loves their job. (Feel free to write them and ask them about it.)

I want you to have the same experience.

Once you define your Ideal Client, the next step will be to figure out how to reach them. That is when you move to the question, "Where do I market?"

The answer is simple: market wherever your Ideal Client is. If they are on LinkedIn, then you will become a LinkedIn master. If they are on Twitter, then that's where you should be.

By defining your Ideal Client, marketing becomes a breeze. Instead of one more chore on your to-do list, it is something exciting and fun.

Your Online Presence

Marketing is about your clients. It is not about you. This is something important to keep in mind. Maybe you like a specific design type, but if it's not something that will attract your Ideal Client, then it's not the right thing for your marketing. Maybe you like YouTube, but if your Ideal Client isn't there and prefers Twitter, stick to Twitter!

Social Media

Running successful social media platforms for business is extremely time-consuming. That means that you must choose carefully and wisely, letting your Ideal Client guide you.

Once you choose which social media platform is the best, get out there and start using it as much as you can. Learn everything you can about it—about the algorithms they use and more. You want to become the best that you can be on that platform.

In order to succeed on social media, you must be consistent. You have to constantly show up over and over for it to work. If that means posting daily, then do that. Show up on your Facebook Lives on a consistent time and day so people can count on you.

<u>Website</u>

Your website is important too. If you don't have a website, you don't exist. You cannot rely solely on social media. Social media rules are always changing, and the owners of each platform are the true owners of its information. It's important to have your own space online where you can own the information and space. That's what your website is and needs to be for you.

Your website should be written solely for your Ideal Client. Many lawyers have cookie-cutter websites with similar language instead of focusing on the Ideal Client.

Most people aren't seeking out lawyers because things are going well in their lives. Your clients are overwhelmed by the legal problems they can't solve themselves. When they visit your website, they want to instantly know that you can help them.

Your website should be a response to the questions:

- Can you help me?

- Have you handled this type of case before?

- Are you the right lawyer for me?

Every word on your website should be carefully chosen. Every word should speak directly to your Ideal Client.

For example, the language on the website of a personal injury attorney could be something like:

"We have worked with hundreds of clients who have suffered through the pain and agony of being injured in a car accident. We have helped enable them to get the medical treatment they need and the financial settlements they deserve."

This is a stark contrast to:

"Our firm handles personal injury cases."

Your client might not even know his/her case is called "personal injury." They might think they need a "car accident lawyer." **Speak the language of your clients.** Talk to them in words that *they* would use. Eschew the legal terminology and technical terms. It doesn't serve your clients. Save the legalese for your briefs. Use their words on your website.

Your *About Me* page

The "About Me" on your website is the most important place to showcase who you are, what you do, and your "why."

Most lawyers use the "About Me" to tell which bars they are a member of, what professional organizations they belong to, and more. However, this is not what your Ideal Client wants to know about you!

They want to know what kind of cases you handle, why you do this work, why you care about your clients, and why they should hire you. This is what it is all about.

They need to know why you are the right lawyer for them, and this is where you get to tell them why. It should be personalized and not sound like anyone else's. You can weave in any accolades while focusing on what you do.

Here's my about me, just to give you an idea:

I am a nationally recognized **award-winning** immigration attorney, the founder of Alexandra Lozano Immigration Law and the lead immigration attorney of the firm. My goal is to keep families together and help immigrants remain in the United States. I work in immigration court to help defend my clients from deportation (now called "removal"), including complex deportation cases such as when a client has been convicted of a crime. I also prepare waivers, family-based petitions, Adjustment of Status, Consular Processing, Asylum, citizenship, and visas for victims of crimes (such as the U Visa). I have won many cases before the immigration court, Board of Immigration Appeals, and I have done Oral Arguments before the Ninth Circuit Court of Appeals.

Immigration is my life. My family is a family of immigrants. My husband is from Mexico and we run the law firm together. My kids are all first generation American on their father's side. My grandparents were from Italy and the Czech Republic. My grandmother received asylum in the United States.

I am fluent in Spanish. My entire practice and life is dedicated to the rights of Latinos in the United States and the advancement of the Latino community through the use of the U.S. immigration system. I previously held a prestigious internship at the Seattle Immigration Court (EOIR).

I don't mention:

- what kind of award I won

- where I went to school

- my best-selling book

- my membership group, Six-Figure Solo

They either don't matter or are not directly relevant to my work as an immigration attorney and how I serve my clients. What I wanted to convey was that if you're an undocumented Latino in the United States, I'm the right fit for your legal case and I sincerely care about your situation.

Your "About Me" should elicit the same feeling from your Ideal Client.

Avvo

While Avvo is controversial, you should claim your online profile, because it does help you come up higher in online searches. Make it as comprehensive as you can. The more you fill in, the higher the score they give you.

Google and Yelp

An easy way to be found online is to claim your Google and Yelp Listing. Make sure your address is up to date. Make it really easy when people search for you online. Both Google and Yelp give people a place to rate you and leave reviews. This is great because the more reviews you get, the higher you rank in searches when people search for your name.

Google Ads

Google itself has a wide range of options for helping you rank high when people google lawyers in your area of practice. Google Ads is one of the paid options that can have huge returns for you and your business when done right. As with everything, it takes some experimenting to get it right.

The online space is important and there is a lot to know. Take these different platforms one-by-one, experiment with them, and make them work for you.

Facebook Live for Success

Facebook has catapulted my firm's success. In this section, I will share how I leveraged Facebook Live to create goodwill, increase consultations, and ultimately, turn more profit.

Facebook is a powerful tool for bringing people together. Most everyone's Ideal Client spends a great deal of time on Facebook. That's why it's a great place to reach potential clients and connect with the community you want to serve.

- Use your Facebook business page as a way to have an ongoing and constant conversation with potential, current, past, and future clients.

- Promote your own events for the community such as free legal clinics. You can create an event on your page and pay to boost it.

- Post relevant information memes. Fun and informative.

- Run promotions for free consultations.

I could go on and on about the creative things you can do with Facebook to help build your business, but because Facebook Live has transformed my business, I want to tell you how you can use it to take your business to the next level.

What is Facebook Live?

I'm sure you likely already know, but Facebook Live is a way to talk to your followers live through your Facebook business page. Note that this isn't through your personal page, it's your business page. When you "go live," you will be recording yourself right there in that moment, speaking to your followers.

Don't be scared!

Many lawyers are nervous or scared to go on Facebook Live. They're afraid to make a mistake and look bad.

But when you are on Facebook Live, all you are going to do is talk about the same things you talk about every single day in consultations. This isn't anything new!

Another fear is how they look and sound on camera. I promise you that:

- You look and sound way better than you think.

- The people you serve just want and need your great information. They don't care about how you look. They just care about the information you are there to give.

Two quick makeup tips:

- A strong lip will show better than any other makeup, so use a brightly colored lipstick.

- Contour your face. You'll find various tips for contouring online. It's a simple technique that helps your face look thinner on camera. Those can help you feel more confident while you're filming.

Make a Weekly Show

Consistency is key. Make your Facebook (FB) Live a weekly show where you come on at the same time on the same day. Give your show a name. And get on there, and tell your followers that they can ask you questions.

Tips for a good FB Live every week:

- Write a post, the words that go with the FB Live video, right before going live. Use it to give a description of the episode. I've found it to be a good idea to put in quotes a question that I receive a lot and say, "come ask your questions live! Please invite your friends!". Always include your phone number in the post.

  - An example, "Can I get my papers after being in the US for 10 years?" Lawyer Alexandra Lozano answers this and YOUR questions LIVE right now on #MiAbogadaDice. Please share! 206-406-3068.

- It takes a few minutes before the questions start rolling in, so have some topics ready to discuss *briefly*.

- Your topics should not be overly legal or involve your over-explaining things. You need to make sure that you are brief and to the point.

- Focus on topics involving the case types that will bring you new business—meaning that you will focus on (1) how someone can qualify and (2) what the benefits are to the client for doing that case type.

  - It is going to sound a little bit like a commercial for a lawyer. "Have you been injured in a car accident? Call us!" While it won't be *that* simplistic, it's along those lines.

- Constantly remind people to write in their questions.

- You also need to constantly give your phone number. Each time you answer a question, say something like, "Thank you so much for being here. I truly appreciate your question. I'd love to talk to you about this more. You can call my office for a full consultation at _____."

- The idea is to answer questions *generally*, not in full-depth. You do not need to analyze cases on the spot! For example, if someone asks me "I've been here for 10 years, I don't have a criminal record, and my kids were born here, can I get my papers?" It gives me the opportunity to talk about a widely held myth in the immigrant community about gaining legal status based on your time in the US. I say something like, "Even though there is no way to gain status through the years you have lived here, there may be other options available for you. I think it would be a great idea for you to give us a call to schedule a consultation, because I would really like to look at solutions for you and your family." And then I give my phone number.

  - People *feel* like it is very personalized advice even if it is not.

- You are giving excellent information to the community. For example, that question that I just mentioned is a question I get asked every single time I do a FB Live. It is also a question that I get asked almost every day in consultations. That means that by getting this information out there about this myth, I am empowering the community and changing lives. I am helping people know what is and isn't legally possible for them. It is important.

- If people ask you very detailed, personal questions, or if they ask you a question that you don't know the answer to (yes, this has happened to me before), I like to direct them to a consultation. "Thank you so much for the question. The truth is that this is more complex than I can explain right now, and you deserve a full hour to talk about this in depth. I really recommend that you call the office to schedule a consultation so that I can give your case the time and attention it deserves." Then I give my phone number. (of course!)

- Give disclaimers that you are not giving legal advice, rather that you are providing legal information. I try to do this after every question, but I usually do it after every few questions. I say something as simple as, "Just a reminder that this is general legal information, not legal advice. For legal advice, you need to schedule a consultation."

When the FB Live is Over

Once your FB Live is done, the work is not over yet. Here's what you do next:

- Publish the video to your page. It's just a click of a button when you end the show. That way it will stay on your page, or "live" on your page, when it's done.

- Pin the video to the top of your page.

  - On your post at the top there are three little dots. Click on that, and there's an option to "pin to top." Click on that.

- Boost the post.

- Boosting is a way to pay to have more people see your video.

- It is incredibly important that you create the audience that you want to reach, being as specific as possible.

- When you boost your post, you can make the settings tailored do your Ideal Client. When you boost the post, you can delineate gender, age range, marital status, types of TV shows they like, and more.

- I usually pay about $250 for 7 days of ads or "boost." It will get me one week of "replays" until the next episode of my show.

- When people write comments on the videos, go through all of the comments and "like" them.

- Be sure to respond to each and every comment.

  - I.e. "Thank you for giving me the opportunity to answer your question live. [phone number]"

  - If you didn't get to answer the question live, try to give a super simple, one-sentence response—something like, "Possibly, but I would need to know more to be able to answer that question. Call us for a consultation at [number]."

- Respond to all your inbox messages with a canned answer

  - You are going to get a ton of questions in your inbox asking for free advice. You don't have to answer them all back with individualized information. In fact, you shouldn't. You do not want to create an incorrect illusion of an attorney/client relationship.

  - More than that, rRemember that this is all part of your marketing plan. You are giving out great free information in your FB Lives, so you don't need to do an individualized analysis of each case by messenger. Instead, respond with a canned response directing them to either call your office or to give you their number so that you can call them.

- At first, it feels weird, but if you don't do this, you will drown in your FB page.

- Your goal is to turn browsers into buyers. Your page can give great, free information. If people want more, they can call you to work on their cases.

Got it?

FB Live is really fun once you get into it. When you have people who watch your show weekly and become your fans it becomes even better. Consistency is key to making this work. You must get on every week. I promise you that the more you do it, the easier it gets, the more people you will have watching, and the more you will enjoy it.

Now, get going!

Build and Maintain an Email List

No matter what happens to social media, there's one thing isn't going anywhere: email.

My clientele does not have or use email, so I have had to be really creative with my marketing and use a lot of old-fashioned techniques in addition to relying on social media. But if your Ideal Client is on email, then that's where you need to be.

What Does it Mean to Build an Email List?

All it means is to collect people's email addresses. From there, you use an email marketing software, like MailChimp, Aweber, or Constant Contact, to send out emails.

That's it!

What You Should Email About

Having people's email addresses is a privilege. You are admitted into someone's inbox, so you must respect it and provide information that *they* care about.

- Make sure your emails are relevant to your followers and what people want to hear about from you.

- If there's a case that will likely impact their lives in some way, you can share the news and your comments about it.

- Do not get overly legal about the case or explaining the decision. Instead, focus on what it means for your clients, how it affects their lives, the steps they can take, and how you can help protect them.

Other content that you can share in your emails:

- Videos: 90 seconds or less about topics that your clients care about

- Your Facebook Live videos

- Recent client wins—pictures and things like that

- Philanthropic work your firm is engaged in

- Blogs, articles, or books that might be of interest to the people on your list

Keep the information relevant to *them*.

Start to really pay attention to the emails of thought leaders in other fields. I'm sure you subscribe to other newsletters. Use those emails for inspiration for your own. See the way that they talk to you and engage with you. See the way that they do not use over-technical words from their industries. Instead they talk to you in a way that you understand and that is meaningful to you.

You need to do the same thing.

How to Build Your List

Of course you can build your email list by asking the people who come into your office for consults, your current clients, and past clients to opt-in for emails. But how else can you build the list?

- Every page of your website should have a "subscribe now" form where people can put in their names and email addresses. You can also point them to a subscription page through your social media sites—tell people why they should subscribe, and then get them on the list.

- You can promote your newsletter through your FB Live as well. Tell people to visit your site, and sign up for your newsletter.

- The best way to build your list is by offering freebies. Freebies are free downloads that they get for signing up for your newsletter. Here are some ideas:

    o A free video about a topic that would interest your Ideal Client or a free book or guide for your Ideal Client. You can use Zoom.

    o A free e-book or e-course preview. You can find someone on Fiverr or Upwork for under $500 to help you put together an e-book, format it, and even design the cover for you.

An ebook can also be a way to create an increased revenue stream because you can make some material to offer as freebies, and you can offer other material on your website for sale and promote through your email list. Imagine if you have an ebook that is about 20 pages long on a topic that is relevant to your Ideal Client, you charge $15 for it, and you make money that way. Plus, it's another way for people to realize that they want to work with you—they read some information from you, and then they want to work with you to know more, do more, or have your assistance in their cases.

An e-course can have the same effect. You can offer both free and paid courses with the same idea—you can offer a free course or video for people subscribing to your newsletter. Or you can have courses or videos for download for a fee on your website to help get people on your list—and to make you an authority on the topic.

E-books and e-courses have the benefits of (1) getting people on your list, (2) adding a stream of income, and (3) increasing your visibility as an expert on the subject.

Now this is just scratching the surface because from here you can really get going with an online business by doing things like sales funnels, email marketing campaigns to upsell, and more. But this is a great place to start.

Remember that with your email list, the most important thing is to create content that is engaging and relevant to your subscribers. It is all about them.

Track Your Leads

For many lawyers, throwing $100 at Avvo or Google Ads and calling it done is what they consider marketing.

Hopefully you'll now use other marketing techniques. Whichever one you use, you need to make sure that it is turning into new business for you. You need to:

1. Track your leads

2. Ensure that the leads are bringing in the clients you want

How did people find out about you?

Tracking your leads means to keep track of how people are finding out about you.

Our money and time are precious, so when you invest money and time into a marketing strategy, you need to make sure you're getting returns.

Many of us ask how people heard about us on our intake sheets, but we don't do anything with that information. What I want you to do is start keeping track of that information.

You want to track:

- How many consultations you are doing a month

- The source of each consultation, meaning how they heard about you

- How many new contracts you have a month

- The source of each new contract

These are critical. For example, if you see that you are getting 8 out of 10 consultations from your Google Ads, then that could be a good resource to continue placing your money in.

However, you also want to ensure that those consultations are turning into new contracts. For example, if the majority of your leads come from Google Ads, yet very few of them are signing up for new contracts, that is something that you want to know as well.

Are you getting qualified leads?

You want "qualified leads." If you get a ton of people in the door for consultations but they aren't turning into new contracts, then they are leads, but they are not "qualified leads." You want to ensure that people are hiring you and that you're getting your Ideal Clients in the door.

You will never know which sources are bringing in the most new consultations and the most new contracts unless you track them. Often when we try to guess what brings in the most people, we are wrong. It's interesting how we have beliefs about things in our business that are completely unsupported by evidence—like if we don't pre-charge for consultations, we often inflate the number of people who actually show up and play down the number of no-shows. This is not intentional. We really believe it. Without any data, though, we can't be sure. That's why it is important to track things in your law firm.

The Right Clients Are in the Right Places

The right clients are extremely important to your overall satisfaction with your firm. This goes back to the idea that your Ideal Client is more than "someone who can pay." Your Ideal Client is someone with whom you enjoy working and serving. They are the clients that you want.

For example, Avvo and Google are not the places that my clients are finding me. They aren't online anywhere except for Facebook.

Once I realized that my Ideal Client was on Facebook, I decided to maximize Facebook as much as I could. And it has been wildly successful for me because now I get the cases I *love*. I do not have one case right now that I don't enjoy.

Figuring out who the right clients are will make you fall in love with your practice again *if* you ensure that you are bringing them in.

While getting new business is great, getting the right business is best. By tracking your leads *and* ensuring that they are bringing in the clients you want to serve, you will be able to find a new level of success in your firm—both professionally and personally.

Workbook

Now it's your turn! Go to page 17 of the Workbook and fill out the exercises for Chapter 1. Visit: http://bit.ly/LFBS-Book

Chapter 7: Client Experience

Clients Are the Heartbeat of Your Law Firm

Clients are the most important part of your law firm. Without them, you don't have a law firm. You don't have a business.

One of the biggest mistakes that lawyers make is constantly complaining about and bad-mouthing clients to our staff. Once we start doing this:

- It sets the wrong tone.

- Our staff also begin to treat the clients with less respect.

- It makes it acceptable to be snappy with clients on the phone or in person.

- Customer service takes a nosedive.

Starting today, right now, it's time to make a change. Treat your clients as what they are, the most important part of your law firm. They literally pay your salary and the salary of your team.

That means both in your firm and outside of your firm. Don't vent about them in an online lawyer forum. Don't joke about them in a negative way anywhere. It will elevate your firm and your client experience.

Creating the best client experience

You can be the best lawyer in the world and get the best results, but if you didn't give clients an excellent experience, they will be less likely to refer people to you in the future. They will be happy for the results, but they will not be happy about their experience with your firm.

Focus all your efforts on creating the best client experience and honoring your clients at every single step of the process. This is of the utmost importance.

Clients Are Facing Their Fears

Don't forget, your clients are scared. Even if they don't act like it. Even if they don't show it. **They are overwhelmed by a problem they don't know how to solve.**

As the lawyer, you know the solution, and you know how the process will go. You can see it step-by-step in your mind. You aren't worried about the outcome because most of the time you know what the outcome will be. But your clients don't know and they are worried.

When they give you a hard time, question what you are doing, or accuse you of not doing anything for them, it's because they are afraid.

When we use that lens, it makes it easier to understand them.

And when we put it all into focus and recognize that clients are the heartbeat of our law firm, then we will use any difficult moments as customer service opportunities. We can listen better and empathize more.

It is easy to lose sight of the client experience while we're busy in the lawyer experience. We are thinking of all of the lawyer things we have to do, the arguments we need to make, and our never-ending tasklist. But it is important to pause, put ourselves on the other side of the desk, and walk through every experience in our law firm from the client's perspective and side.

Have a meeting with your team and stress to them how important your clients are.

- No one is allowed to complain about or bad-mouth a client.

- Begin to tell every single client how important his or her case is to you.

    o Tell them that you want them to win their cases, be protected against future issues, or whatever else it may be.

    o Make sure your team does the same.

    o You likely think it is a given—of *course* you want a great outcome for your clients. But without saying it, the client honestly may not know.

By making these small changes, customer service will increase tremendously. Clients will feel valued and important, which is how they need to feel when they are going through any sort of legal process.

Overcommunication with Clients

How many times do you hear clients say, "You never call me!" How many calls and emails do you get asking for updates in a client's case?

One of the biggest complaints clients have is that they don't hear from their lawyers. Clients are desperate to be communicated with, and for some reason, us lawyers are not great at communicating with them.

We are busy with the legal work. We believe that when we have something to tell them, we will. Otherwise, we keep working.

If a case is pending and just waiting for the next step, we feel like there is nothing to talk about. I used to believe that if I was calling a client to say, "There are no updates in your case right now, all is going well," they would be annoyed and wonder why I was calling. But I was wrong.

Clients want to hear from you. As much as you can possibly communicate with them. They want to be over-communicated with.

When you initiate communications with clients, it increases client satisfaction *and* decreases client calls. One of the reasons why we've established an over-communication policy in our law firm is because we wanted to cut down on the constant phone calls of, "What is going on in my case?"

Before I understood anything about customer service, I had a husband-and-wife client. The wife called me weekly to check in on their case. I had learned through my previous law firms that if a client calls that much, she is high-maintenance and annoying and to treat her as such. I would get snappy with this woman on the phone and threatened to charge her by the hour if she kept calling so much. Then the government made a mistake in their case, and I had to meet with them in person to tell them about it.

The wife had tears in her eyes when she said to me, "I am not trying to bother you when I call. It's just that this is our lives, and this is very important to us. All we want is to hear from you."

I was crushed. I had failed to see the client experience. This woman was not high-maintenance, she was stressed and worried. She was overwhelmed. Her and her husband's lives were on the line. I was looking at everything from my side of the desk and not from hers. I had adopted the previous bad examples from law firms I worked at instead of being authentic and client-honoring. I vowed, from then on, I would change things. I never wanted a client to feel like that again. At that moment I decided that I would figure out a way to over-communicate with clients.

Over-communication is easier than you think.

General Monthly Case Update Letters

By sending a monthly letter or email to every client, you can make them feel informed an updated about their cases.

I like to call these a "general" letter because they do not go into the specifics on the client's case.

Instead, you either state that the case is Active, Pending, or Waiting on the Client.

We have codes in our firm—letters in front of each client's name—to indicate that the case is Active, Pending, or Waiting on the Client. Our admin just needs to email everyone on the active list that the case is active, everyone on the pending list that it's pending, and if we are waiting on the client, just that we are waiting on the client. That's it.

This monthly email or letter alone will make your clients feel very nurtured. You are going to be getting in front of the, "What's going on in my case?" phone calls.

In fact, once you make it a habit, if for some reason you don't do it one month, you will immediately see the increase in calls inquiring about how a case is going.

While this does take some work and concerted effort, if you do nothing else in terms of overcommunication then your clients will be much more satisfied.

Specific Monthly Case Update Letters

For certain case types that have processing times that you can update, send specific monthly case update letters telling clients about case processing times.

If there are other specific case types that require updated information on a monthly basis, draft those up so that they can be easily updated monthly.

You can also include the case status checklist, or some sort of infographic, to show where you are in a case and indicate what the next steps are.

Monthly Phone Calls

Try to call every single client every single month to give them updates on their cases. I timed my calls, and they take an average of 90 seconds. If you do a little each day, you can get through them rather quickly.

Client Phone Meetings

One of the biggest forms of client dissatisfaction comes from unreturned phone calls. Most of us lawyers are terrible about returning phone calls, because there are always other things that seem more important to do with our time. So it's hard to get back to the phone calls.

An easy fix to it is this is, instead of your team taking a message and you having to call the client back, have them schedule a formal phone meeting with you for 15 minutes. This way it's on your calendar, and you can be prepared for the meeting by reviewing your notes beforehand.

What I love about doing this 15-minute phone meeting:

- You aren't interrupted in the middle of the work day.

- It doesn't put the burden on you to remember to call them back.

- It takes away the negative charge of a client interaction. For example, if a client calls for a case update, it can often feel like an attacking phone call and we are on the defensive. Part of it is that we are flustered, because we were in the middle of other things and part of it is that we take it personally when clients call to ask how things are going in the case. But if you do the scheduled phone meeting, it makes it a neutral interaction. Actually, it makes it a formal interaction between you and the client, because it's a meeting and it's more than a phone call.

- It's a quick way to improve your response time and increase client satisfaction.

Also, I don't like to do these calls during the middle of the day when I could have a money-making appointment, such as a consultation or client sign up, so instead I designed an hour each day when I am not in the office, 9am–10am, as the set time that my team can schedule the phone meetings.

They don't have to ask me if I am available each time they want to set a call. They know that if anyone wants a phone appointment, it can be scheduled during that one-hour slot Monday through Friday.

Once you get the template letters written and get a process in place for scheduling the phone calls, you will be able to over-communicate with your clients like a pro!

Don't Do Favors for Clients

One of the quickest ways for you to become dissatisfied with your clients is to do favors for them. Though this was discussed this above, it is worth mentioning again.

Let me give you an example. A client asks if you are open on Saturdays, and you say no, but then he tells you how he can't get there during the week and to please meet him on Saturday. You give in. You decide to do the client a favor and go in on a Saturday. You make childcare arrangements. You rearrange your weekend schedule. You show up, and then your client never comes. When you call the client, he says that he got called into work and couldn't make it.

Then you get mad. You did this client a *favor*. You did all this just for *him*, because he asked you to, and because he was desperate.

These situations happens a lot:

- Cutting your fees or leaving out expenses

- Making unfavorable payment plans (i.e. $100 a month instead of the $500 a month you proposed)

- Doing work before being paid ("Can you get started? I will hire you... just get started and I'll pay you in a week."),

- And more

There's no reason to do a client a favor!

This advice was revolutionary to me. In one of the lawyers' groups I'm a part of, a lawyer was complaining about how she did a client a favor, and then the client failed in his responsibility somehow. A bunch of lawyers responded with similar experiences.

And then, a well-respected lawyer wrote, "I don't do clients favors. Period. If they want me to come in on a Saturday, they pay for it. If they want consultations after hours, they pay for it. It's that simple."

When she wrote this, I was floored. She was right, it was simple, but at the same time it was hard from a mindshift perspective.

Doing Favors is a Lose-Lose Situation

Doing favors breeds resentment and frustration. You resent the other person for not responding or appreciating the favor you did for them. The other person resents you, because they didn't ask for a favor, they just wanted representation.

Your frustration will flow through your firm and your team and will affect everyone's interactions with the clients. It isn't fair for anyone. It's a lose-lose situation.

Once things start going this way, it will erode the trust that you've built with your clients. Then when hiccups happen in cases—that are not your fault or that are the result of things that are out of your control—clients will feel like you did it on purpose, or that you let it happen because you don't care. I'm telling you, it sounds crazy, but it isn't. This truly happens.

There is no reason to do a favor for a client. A client is a client and a lawyer is a lawyer. Clients pay a lawyer to do a job. They aren't asking you to do a favor. They are asking you to do your job to the maximum, and they pay you a fair fee for it.

Lay Down the Terms

When clients ask you to do things for them, and they aren't things that you would normally do (such as meeting on a Saturday), but you decide to do them as a "favor" to the client, the ironic part is that clients don't think they are asking you to do a favor.

We have to go back to the fact that most people have never worked with a lawyer before. They don't know how it works. They need you to help teach them how to work with a lawyer. They may just think that you are available when a client needs you because that's what they are paying you for.

Help them understand what is reasonable and what isn't and what's within the scope of your representation and what isn't.

It will surprise you what happens when you start to say that you have to charge for "extras."

For example, when potential clients call and say they can only meet on weekends or evenings, and you say that you can do a consultation on an evening or weekend for $500, but your weekday rate for a consultation is $150, it's amazing to see how people are suddenly able to make their schedules work with yours.

The goal of running a successful law firm is to be able to enjoy your firm and enjoy your life. That's the whole point. When you stop doing favors for clients, you will instantly find more satisfaction with your work, your firm, and your client interactions.

Honoring the Client Experience

Your client entrusted you with something important in her life. She also invested money into you and your firm. That should never be taken for granted.

We can get so lost in all the legal work that it can be hard to honor the client experience in every single thing that we do in our firms.

To do this, see every single interaction with your firm from the perspective of the client. You may need to ask friends or relatives to assist with this. Go through the client's interactions with your firm:

- Initial phone call

- Initial in-office consultation

- Sign up appointment

- Follow-up appointments

- Calls about case

- Case closure

- Post-case closure

See how each of these processes make you feel.

- How are you treated based on your firm's policy and procedures?

- Do you feel like you are a transaction?

- Do you feel like you matter to the lawyer? To the law firm?

- Do you feel like you are getting what you paid for?

Are the lawyer and the law firm meeting your expectations? What could be done better? Or differently?

Again, it may be hard to see this neutrally as yourself. When we did this in our firm, we realized some of the following things. I'm sharing them with you to help you think critically about your own firm:

- No one ever called the client from the firm number. Everyone was calling from personal extensions which didn't even look similar to the firm number. It caused a lot of confusion for clients who had 3-4 different phone numbers for the firm.

- Calls were short, often curt. There was no nurturing in the call. The calls were to set appointments and give very straightforward information. If people wanted to give background on their cases, they were cut off and told that if they wanted to talk about that, they needed to schedule a consultation with the lawyer.

- Every interaction with the client was different depending on who they talked to both on the phone and in the office.

- Case turnaround times were long.

- Clients were only called about their cases to communicate news.

- Phone calls and emails were not returned in a timely manner.

- There was disorganization in the way that we asked for documents from clients.

- The frame that held my law school diploma in my office was run-down looking and scratched up, as were the frames of the other certificates. I didn't notice.

- There were often stacks of papers that I "needed to get to" in my office.

- There were old magazines stacked around my office for clients, despite the fact that clients never read them and neither did I.

These are just a few things!

But, with the help of others, I was able to see these things with fresh eyes. The great thing is that we were able to take quick action to make everything better. Nothing was so huge that it was unfixable. And it won't be for you either. But you can't change it if you don't see it.

The goal is to honor the clients and their investments in your firm with their money and their trust. Here are a few steps you can take right now and a few questions to consider to honor the client experience more deeply:

Phones

- Before answering the phone, let it ring once. Smile, breathe, and then answer.

- Have a script on how to answer the phone to make sure that that experience is uniform no matter who answers.

- Never cut off someone who is calling. Let them tell their stories. Let them speak without interrupting. Be reassuring, and use great customer service.

- When someone wants to schedule a consultation, do not simply throw out the price. Instead, uses sales techniques to sandwich the price in between the benefits.

- Have a protocol for how current client calls will be handled. For example, if a client asks to speak with a lawyer, what steps need to be taken before the call can go through to a lawyer? Also, have a process and procedure for returning calls.

In-Office Meetings and Appointments

- Create scripts for how clients are greeted and treated during a consultation as well as in-office meetings.

- Determine the look that you want to exude during the meeting. For a more professional look, simply add a suit jacket.

- Take a look around your office. Is there anything that looks old, dingy, or worn down? Does it need to be tidied up? What could be done to elevate the look of your office?

- What is the language and tone you are using?

- What is your communication style? Are you over-explaining things? Are you joking around too much? How can you be more direct and clear with your clients?

- Are you providing clients with visual aids?

Client Contact Throughout the Case

- How often are clients hearing from you? In which ways?

- What phone numbers are they receiving calls from?

- How quickly are calls and emails returned?

- Is there something that you can do to improve communication throughout the case?

- Looking at it from the client's perspective, do you think he feels like he hears from you enough? Think about it, for your client, his case is the only case that matters. Look at it as if you were that particular client. Would it feel like your case mattered? Would it feel like you were important?

- How can you improve client contact today?

- How do you celebrate a case that ends with a positive resolution? Do you send a gift? Send a letter?

- Do you send an email newsletter? How often? Is the content engaging?

- Do you send a "hello" check-in every quarter with current and past clients? (Such as an email newsletter, postcard, or something exciting and different.)

- From the perspective of one client, only one, do you believe that that client feels communicated with to a level of satisfaction?

Unique and Memorable Client Experience

What details separate you from the rest? For example, do you offer your clients something to drink? How do you bring it to them? Do you serve it on a tray or a silver platter? Can you create a drink menu to provide to your clients? Or maybe a self-serve beverage area.

Do you have a special drink for kids? Toys for kids to play with?

By addressing these small details, from the look and feel of your office to the little ways that you can help a client feel more comfortable throughout the experience, you will show your clients how much they matter to you, both personally and professionally.

It's also a contribution to your brand uniqueness. You know how certain phone companies are so notorious for their horrible or stellar customer service? Customer service is part of your trademark!

How to Handle the Phones

As lawyers, we rarely think of our firms as a place where customer service is at the forefront- we normally think our legal expertise is at the forefront. We think we're already doing excellent service to our clients with our legal work. However, we have to think like the client. In addition to great legal work, which many people can do, they need excellent customer service, which is something that will be unique to you and your firm.

The phones are where customer service is at the highest level of importance. The phones provide the very first contact that people have with your law firm. They are likely nervous, scared, and overwhelmed.

Most people have never called a lawyer before. They don't know what to expect. Also, they have probably researched a lot of lawyers and finally decided on you. Part of the call is to see if you are the right lawyer for them.

If you think about it from that perspective, how should the phones be answered? That person should be nurtured and treated with the highest level of care.

Here are some customer service tips for the initial phone call:

- Initial phone call is a pitch

    - This means that you are trying to sell the person on coming for a consultation. The entire call should be all about that.

- Never interrupt

    - Oftentimes when they call, they want to tell the person who answers the phone about their case. Let them. Do not interrupt them.

- Say their name at least three times

    - Ask for their name in the beginning of the transaction, and be sure to use it throughout the call.

- Reflect their feelings

- Reflecting their feelings means to echo back what you are hearing from them. "It sounds like this is a stressful time for you." Or, "It sounds like you are overwhelmed looking for a lawyer." Or, "I can see why this is difficult for you."

- We all want to feel acknowledged and important. We all want to feel cared for. By reflecting the feelings of the caller, you show them that they are important.

- Show compassion

  - One of the main things that people want to know when they are hiring a lawyer is that you care about them and their case. Most of us think that it is a given—we do this work because we care. We obviously want to help. But it isn't as obvious as you would think. It's important to say it. Tell them with words how much you care.

  - If they are starting a new business, and they need a lawyer to help them get started, you can say something like, "Congratulations on your new business! That's so exciting! We can definitely help you get set up."

  - If they have a family member in jail, then you can say something like, "It sounds like you are going through a difficult time. I am so sorry to hear it. I can schedule a consultation with the lawyer so she can visit your family member with the hopes that we can help."

- Offer your unique competitive advantage

  - Work in what makes you different during that phone call. "Going through the immigration process is very stressful. Everyone in our office has gone through it personally, so we understand. We want to support you during this difficult time."

  - Or, "The lawyer in our office works with cases exactly like yours. She has a lot of experience with [case type], and I know that she will be able to help you with what you need."

  - You and your team should be able to put into words what makes you different.

- Thank the caller

  - Make sure to use his or her name. "Thank you for calling, Mayra. We look forward to seeing you soon."

Avoid Negative Words

There are some words that trigger negative feelings and experiences. This has been studied. And sales masters avoid the negative words so that they can close deals. Most of the negative words are just normal words that we use when talking about transactions that include money. We don't even notice them!

Here is a list of the "negative words" and what to say instead.

Don't say:	Instead say:
1. Cost	-Worth & value
2. Down payment investment	-Initial
3. Monthly payment investment	-Monthly
4. Problem	-Challenge
5. You should	-We should
6. Sign authorize	-Approve or
7. Speaking to	-Talking with
8. But	-And
9. Make sense	-Sound to you

10. Always say: *because*

You can see that it all comes down to expressing things in terms of value. For example, when people hire you for a legal case, they aren't just paying money like a car payment. Rather, they are investing in their futures. They are investing in fixing their legal problems or finding solutions to protect themselves and their families in some way.

The word "problem" feels like something insurmountable. The word "challenge" makes it feel like something we can overcome.

Also, you will likely notice that on the negative words list it is about "you," and the positive side makes it "we." This helps emphasize the fact that you are on the client's team. You will be in it together. It's not just about resolving that person's legal issue, it's about getting results together.

Role Play

The client calls and says she wants to explain the entire case, "Let me just tell you a little bit about my situation."

The client says that he wants to know if he qualifies before he schedules the consultation.

The client says that he can't believe you charge for a consultation. Other lawyers don't do that!

Watch this video to see the role play for each scenario here: https://youtu.be/CDYp51wqkBA

Add in Special Touches

A way to wow your clients and to make an impact is to do little things that can have a big impact on them.

When I was on a non-profit board, we had a fundraiser training that changed the way I see nurturing clients. They said that every single month there needs to be a "touch" of the donors.

Those touches don't mean asks. They are reminders about the work we do as an organization and ways to engage the donors more. The same can go for a for-profit business that wants to have ongoing business with their current, past, and potential clients.

Most lawyers treat their clients as transactions and nothing more. Even lawyers who care deeply about their clients and who put their hearts and souls into working for their clients often fail to cultivate the client relationship. Most of us don't think that we are treating our clients as transactions, because we care so much. But our actions speak differently. The good news is, that's easy to change!

There are small things that you can do to let the clients know that you are thinking about them!

Weekly Newsletter

A weekly emailed newsletter is just an email with the latest about your firm, your area of practice, or something that might interest your current, past, and potential clients.

You can create this using something like MailChimp or Constant Contact or some other type of email newsletter software. It doesn't take very long, especially once you get a template set up and started.

It's a fast and easy way for clients to hear from you. Also, it is an important way to establish name recognition with your clients. You want to be something more to them than a transaction. You want to be the first name they think of when their friends or family need a lawyer in the future. Keep yourself fresh in their minds with a weekly newsletter.

If you do weekly FB Live videos or write a blog, you can use your weekly newsletter to promote it.

Thank You Note

Sending a short thank you note, whether by mail or by email, is a great way to thank a client for coming in to your office for a consultation. We had postcards made with Vistaprint, which are cheap to make and cheap to mail, and we send them out to our clients. It's just as easy to have an email sent after they leave your office saying, "Thank you for your consultation, if you need anything, we are here to serve you!"

By using email, you can also schedule a follow up email to check in again about a week later. This is another "touch."

Sign Up Gift

Spoil your clients! Thank them for signing up with your law firm by giving them a gift at sign up. The key is for it to be branded—bring in your logo and your tag line. You want to give them something special that they can use *and* be reminded of your firm and your great work.

You can give them the gift right at sign up, or you can mail it to them as an additional touch a few days after they have met with your firm.

New Year's Gift

Almost everyone sends a gift at the winter holidays, so make yourself stand out by waiting until the New Year to send something out to your clients. We like to send a branded calendar that is either a tear-off calendar or a calendar magnet that can go on the fridge. But you can send anything that you think would be meaningful and useful to your current and past clients.

Change of Seasons Greeting

Each change of season is an opportunity to reach out to your current, past, and potential clients. We send out a postcard that says, "Happy Spring," or something along those lines. You can do the same through email. It just is another way to keep yourself top-of-mind for your clients and to say hello.

Birthday Cards

By sending clients a birthday card, and, as a bonus, sending your clients' kids birthday cards, you can create a very meaningful "touch." Whenever we send out birthday cards, clients call to say thank you. They are really appreciative of it.

An easy way to do the hard mailing cards is to send out an entire month's birthday cards on the first of the month. That way the whole month is covered, and you don't have to do any figuring out.

Some email systems, such as Constant Contact, allow you to put in the clients' birthdays and then they will automatically send out an email to the clients.

Case Closing Gift

When you successfully end a case, it's a great time to give a last gift to a client! It can be something that is along the lines of your area of practice or something else that is meaningful and branded. The sky is the limit! The higher the price of the case, the nicer the gift you can give.

Thank You Gifts

Oftentimes, there are people or organizations that send a lot of referrals your way. As a token of your appreciation, you can send a gift, such as a gift basket, a gift card, or something of the like. I know that some bars say that you cannot pay for referrals, which is not what I am suggesting. Rather, once a year or so, saying thank you to the people who have sent referrals your way is a great way to reach out and show your appreciation. Of course, always be sure to be in compliance with your ethics rules.

Workbook

Now it's your turn! Go to page 18 of the Workbook and fill out the exercises for Chapter 1. Visit: http://bit.ly/LFBS-Book

Chapter 8: Efficiency & Systems

Take Yourself Out of the Middle of Your Law Firm

In my work with solo practitioners and small firms throughout the country, I hear over and over that they are completely drained.

- They feel like they are constantly working without a break.

- Tons of time is spent at the office, but things are never getting done.

- They spend most of their days putting out fires and are barely able to get to case work—so they have to do case work after hours: nights and weekends.

- There are so many distractions during the day: phone calls, clients stopping in, staff who have questions, and more.

Without efficient systems in your firm, you are going to be a prisoner to interruptions.

The overarching goal of having a systems-based law firm is to run with consistent results and client experiences. A huge part of attaining that goal comes down to you getting out of the way.

If you are like most solo practitioners, your law firm would crumble without you. You likely could not go on a two-week vacation and have your firm still standing—or perhaps you could, but you would have to be working the entire time and "on" or "available" to your staff pretty much all day, every day.

Does this sound familiar?

- You are the keeper of information in your law firm.

- You know where the files go and how they are organized. You know the latest information in a client's case.

- You know how to prepare a fedex label, where the dropoff is, and the latest dropoff times.

- You know how to file things online with the court or opposing counsel.

- You know how much a client has paid and how much he owes, or at least you are the one who could find out that information.

I worked with a lawyer who would wake up in the middle of the night and make lists of things she needed to do, clients she realized she didn't have files for, and more. She had notebooks filled with pages of things to do. She could barely sleep. She was tormented by anxiety and panic attacks, even while she was sleeping, because she always felt like she was forgetting something. This is an incredibly common experience for law firm owners, because everything relies on you and your memory.

When you're the keeper of information in your firm, you will never, ever, ever be free from your firm. You will run yourself into the ground or into a nervous breakdown if you keep this up.

Right now you are the sun in the middle of the solar system—everything depends on you for survival. It's time to change that.

If you don't think it's possible, I am here to tell you that it is. And in this chapter I will teach you how.

Training Manual

The first step to taking yourself out of the middle of your law firm is this: **Make everything you know, all the information you keep in your head, accessible to everyone in the law firm.**

There has to be one centralized place where *everyone* can go for information. And that place is a living, breathing document that should be the center of your law firm: your training manual.

This document will be the sun in your solar system so that you don't have to be.

Your law firm already has systems and processes. You have ways of doing things, from mail handling to opening and closing cases.

If you don't have things written down, you are constantly training people. CONSTANTLY.

Yes, you. Most staff of solos and small firms just go straight to the attorney when they have questions. This takes up your time. This takes away money. This is the antithesis of efficiency.

You can change this all *today* with a training manual. Though we talked about it a bit before, I want to go through this again in more detail here.

How to setup your training manual

- Email your staff and say that one week from today, you want bullet points of everything they work on—it doesn't matter how small the task is, you want it written down in a bullet point.

  o If you don't have staff, then I want you to do this yourself.

- Every single thing that gets done in your firm needs to go on this list.

  o Then, after you get those lists, make one master list.

- You and your staff are going to document everything that gets done in your firm, step-by-step.

  o Everyone in your firm should do this. Each of your staff has processes on how they do things, and those processes need to be written down.

- Write the steps down as you do them. That way it flows naturally, and you ensure that you get everything in there.

- Give everyone—including yourself—*deadlines* to get this done.

- Test the steps. Get family members or friends who aren't part of the firm or who don't know how to work in a law firm to try to follow the steps. Have them come in and follow your training manual, and see how it goes.

  o What steps need to be modified, added to, etc?

  o This is very important! You need to make sure everything is in there *and* check the steps to make sure they work for you.

- As you grow, you might adapt to new technologies or develop new ways of doing things. Just keep updating the training manual to make sure everything is documented there.

The goal is for anyone to be able to walk into your law firm without needing to ask anyone how to do any of the tasks they are assigned. They could just pick up the training manual and figure it out.

Though this does take some work to put together, it is worth it. Your life will be transformed, I promise you. This is the first huge step that you can take toward not being the center of your law firm.

It helps staff with communications, both internally, within your law firm, and externally, between your firm and your clients.

Communication Inside Your Firm

Because you have been the keeper of information at your law firm, you are constantly interrupted. People ask you all day long about cases, files, administrative tasks, "how tos," and more. This has to stop. Today.

"Stop Asking the Lawyer" Policy

You might have an open-door policy within your firm. But an open-door policy is your staff being able to reach out to you, not a free-for-all so that people can come and interrupt you all day long with questions that they should figure out for themselves!

Everyone should be looking to the manuals and *not* asking you pretty much anything. All the information should be in your training manual and policy manual. Include this: what to do if someone does not know how to do something or the answer to something.

I am not kidding. Include the steps for finding out information that someone might need help figuring out.

Ours is something like:

- First check the training manual.

- If it isn't there and it is information that you could find with a Google search, do that next.

- If it is more of an in-office procedural question, then ask a certain person (name the person). Before asking them the question, you need to be able to describe the efforts that you've taken to figure out the answer yourself.

- If that person cannot answer the question, then the question goes to [another person]. As a very last resort, the question goes to the lawyer. This means that there is no possible other way of finding out this information except for asking the lawyer.

These need to be included in your training and policy manuals and they should be implemented without exceptions.

The other important step: STOP answering everyone's questions.

In my firm, this is so embedded in the culture that if any of the staff asks another something that he could find out with a little bit of effort on his part, the other staff member will call them out on it. No one takes shortcuts by asking someone else the answer. Everyone has to learn by doing and figuring out on his or her own.

If you do not take a hard line on this then it will never change.

Handling Case-Related Questions

1. All client-related communications, meaning questions they have, information they tell the assistant that they want the lawyer to know, etc, have to be communicated to the lawyer through the case management system *exclusively*. (Note that this means not in person and not via email.)

2. All case-related questions during case preparation are communicated via sticky notes.

Number one here is simple, and we will talk about this more in this chapter about case management systems.

However, it is critical to note that there is no reason why you should *ever* be orally told important client information nor should it be chatted to you via Gchat or any other internal communication platform in your firm.

Messaging through your case management system is the only way.

Number two is my favorite tip: Communicate via sticky notes. Yes it sounds funny, and it also sounds almost too simple to be a real suggestion, but this will change your life.

Instead of asking you, the assistant sticks a sticky note on the page where he has the question and writes the question there. Usually the question is, "Is that right?" Seriously that is usually the question. Or if there is something he wants me to see, he writes, "Is this okay to include?" or even "Include?" It's that simple.

You also respond with sticky notes. You write yes or no, or you ask them to call the client to clarify something.

If there is something that you find missing from the packet, instead of talking to your assistant about it, write a sticky note that explains what you want/need from the client or the packet and stick it on the top. Or, if you've reviewed everything and it's ready to go, stick a sticky note on top that says "ready."

This one tip is going to get hours back in your day and your team's day and allow you to be more productive. It is game-changing.

Formal Case Review

Formal case review is important because you can have your entire team come together to check in on the status of cases, know what is going on, and assign tasks just to ensure that nothing is missing or falling through the cracks.

What we did to make our case reviews more efficient is have everyone bring their computers. They all have their case management systems up and open so they can easily review their notes in the cases as needed. It has made the case review about one hour despite having several hundred open cases.

Cases that Need Extra Help

There are some cases that are trickier and more complex and can't be discussed in a case review or through sticky notes... but this is rare and should be the exception. If you think that this describes the majority of your cases, then it is a sign that your systems are not yet tight enough. (Don't worry though, they will be by the time you end this chapter.)

However, in the event that this is the case, you need to schedule a formal 15-minute meeting with your assistant. It needs to be put on the calendar and kept to 15 minutes only. You should be able to handle any and all questions and concerns during that time in order for the case to be completed.

If you don't schedule the appointment then it is easy for it to get pushed off for other work—which means that it could cause a delay in filing the case. Also, if you don't schedule it for a certain amount of time, it could end up taking much longer, because it's easy to go off on tangents and discuss unrelated issues. It is important to remain focused to make sure that you maximize time for both you and your team.

Stop Going Into Your Team's Offices!

Something I did for a long time was to go into my assistants' offices to drop something off or pick something up or ask a question or let them ask me a question. But what I didn't realize was how disruptive and inefficient it was for them—just the same way it is for us lawyers when we are constantly getting interrupted.

So I stopped doing it. Usually when I come in in the morning, my desk is filled with cases for my review. My team drops the cases off on my desk before I get into to the office. I review them and then message the assistant that they are all ready for her, so she comes and picks them up when she has a free moment.

Do you see how this works to ensure that she gets the files without interrupting what she is doing?

We also have other ways of getting the files back and forth. For example, we will place them on the business manager's desk, because we both pass there a lot, so it is a drop-off and pick-up point that works well for us that doesn't involve interrupting anyone.

You can and should do the same. Try to implement this today. See how it works and how it feels for you. It does feel weird at first. It does feel a bit cold at first. But you will see that once it gets rolling, everyone on your team, including you, will have high levels of satisfaction.

With these processes, you empower your team to take actions on their own. You maximize your time and your team's time by streamlining the way that questions are handled. You make efficiency one of the core values of your law firm.

Apply the same efficiency to everything else, especially to cases and client management.

Start the Case at Sign Up

One of the primary ways that lawyers continue to perpetuate inefficiency in their law firms comes from the way that sign-ups are handled. Most lawyers and law firms have a sign-up appointment in which they sign a contract with the client and then, in that meeting, tell the client what's needed to start the case.

Most often that sign-up appointment puts the burden on the client to get back in touch when she has all of the documents ready to begin the case.

This is where things start to go south for many reasons:

- You and your team become the client's babysitter. You have to constantly track the client down to see how it is coming with the documents.

- You wait on the client to make the next move, and the client is likely waiting on you to make the next move.

- Client satisfaction decreases the longer a lawyer is retained without filing a case. *They feel this way regardless of whether the delay is the client's fault or not.*

- Clients often feel overwhelmed by the amount of information that they need to provide, and then they end up not getting it to you, or getting it to you in an incomplete manner, which again puts you back on the cycle of you waiting on the client while the client thinks that she is waiting on you, and so forth.

There are ways that you can turn this around right now to make things faster and more efficient and to increase client satisfaction right away.

Give the Document List at the Consult

Instead of waiting for the sign-up appointment to give clients the list of information and documents that you will need from them, give them the list in the consultation.

I already discussed the benefits of the document list in "Chapter 4: Sales." Page back to that if needed for reference.

Making your case sign-ups more efficient not only increases client satisfaction and case turnaround times, it increases your income too.

Have Questionnaires Prepared by Case Type

After the sign up and payment, instead of having the client leave and come back for another appointment to get started, get started right there in that moment.

The way to do this is by creating questionnaires that have every single piece of information that you need from clients.

Here's where you veer away from the inefficient norm:

- **Fill out the questionnaire with the client right then and there.**

Don't let them bring it home and wait for them to turn it in. Sit there and ask the client every single question so that way you are done all in one shot.

Will there be information that the client needs that she doesn't have on hand? Sometimes. But that can be supplemented. Instead of worrying about that, focus on getting as much of the information as you possibly can from the client in that moment.

In that sign-up appointment, you'll get all or almost all of the information and documents that you need in order to prepare the case.

Follow-Up Appointment

Set a follow-up appointment date one to two weeks later for the client to come in to sign the forms or complete anything else that they need to complete for the case.

At that follow-up appointment, the goal is to have done 100% of every single thing you can possibly do for the case. That means that your legal argument is written, your cover letter is put together, your forms are done. Everything on your end is completely done for the case by that date.

By having the questionnaires completed at the sign-up and providing the document list in the consultation, it is usually really easy to be able to do this.

We have a coding system for cases in our firm: Active, Pending, or Waiting on the Client. Our goal is that when the client comes in a week or two after the sign-up appointment, the case either becomes Pending or it can be called "Waiting on the Client," because we are 100% ready with our part.

Sometimes people sign up on the spot, so they won't have all of the documents with them. That's fine—you can do the questionnaire anyway. Get everything done that you can get done. And then you have the follow-up appointment scheduled for them to come in. They can (1) bring in the documents at that appointment, (2) email or fax the documents over ahead of time, or (3) drop by the office before the next appointment to deliver the documents.

It is really easy when you tell the client that you will be ready to submit at the next meeting if the client gets all of the docs to you ahead of time.

What if the Client Continues to Fail to Bring the Needed Documents?

- Send email reminders.

- Call the client to remind them.

- In every single contact, remind the client that the case is being delayed because of not having the documents and that you are ready to file, but can't because of missing documents or information.

- Schedule an appointment for your client to come in to the office.

    o Tell him that the purpose of the meeting is to bring in the missing documents. Usually a phone call is enough, but if that isn't working, schedule him with your assistant so your assistant can again go over the needed documents.

    o A 15-minute meeting is sufficient.

- If six months pass, tell the client that you will have to close out the case if they don't respond or that you will have to charge additional fees if they don't respond.

- It is important to push them hard around that six-month mark, because, again, even though they caused the delay, once they get those documents to you, they are going to complain about how long you are taking to get their cases filed. They will say, "You've been my lawyer for eight months, and you haven't done anything for me." And you want to say back, "Well you took six months to get things to me, so technically it's only been two months that you've been waiting for results!" And even though it's true, and even if you said that to the client, it will not change the opinion the client has that this is somehow your fault.

Client delays cause extra work. For example, if the form versions are updated and you have to redo them all, then that is extra work for you. And it's something that is not your fault, since you have had the case ready.

Now that my systems are so tight, with providing the document list at the consultation and the questionnaire at the sign up, we are almost never waiting on documents or information from clients for more than 30 days. They want to move quickly, because they realize that we have moved quickly.

You are all working toward the same goal: the resolution of their legal issue. They want it and you want it so make sure that you regularly express that to them. "I want to submit your case. I am ready, but I am just waiting on you. Let's get this filed! If you get me your documents today, I can file by tomorrow."

The better you are at communicating this, the faster things will move forward.

Keep the Cases Moving Forward

In today's society people are busy, and because legal issues are so stressful, it is easy for people to push them off. That's why I don't believe in giving clients questionnaires or having open-ended due dates for them to turn in documents.

They come to you because they need guidance. They need you to take the lead. So lead them. Keep moving the case forward the best that you can.

Use these systems of a document list at the consultation, questionnaires at the sign up, and calendared next appointments at the date of sign-up, to ensure that cases keep flowing forward.

An added benefit to this system is that your staff can organize themselves around what needs to get done next. They know that next week, Manuel is coming to sign his forms and declaration, which means that it all has to be prepared in time for that meeting—lawyer review and all.

This system prevents cases from being pushed down on the priority list. All cases are handled right when they come in, and then they are submitted and out the door. It makes for a fast turnaround and high satisfaction for clients, staff, and for you as the attorney.

Leveraging a Case Management System

There is NO other way to be organized and efficient

A case management system is a must. Whenever people ask me what I wish I had known or done differently from the beginning, the answer is that I wish I had gotten a case management system. It doesn't matter if you have five cases or 50 cases, you need a case management system today.

I know many lawyers use the inefficient system that I used to use—I made an excel spreadsheet of all of my clients' names. Then in each of their e-files, I made a word document that I would use to take case notes. Some lawyers still take notes by hand and then hard file them. All of this breed inefficiency. You can't access the file easily. Tons of notes—and time—are getting lost in the process.

The only way to keep your cases organized is through a case management system. I don't care how organized you are as a person, there is nothing out there better than a case management system. I only wish I had understood that sooner.

Your Case Management System is the Keeper of Information

Remember how we talked about how you are not supposed to be the keeper of information? Well, the case management system *is* the keeper of information. It is *the* place where *everyone in* your firm can go to know the latest client information. This is critical.

Your case management system will be your "insurance package" against turnover. You will never again depend on one person's knowledge about a case or client. The case management system is where all of that information is going to be stored.

I have read a statistic that most millennials only stay at a job for 18 months. I myself am a millennial (the oldest side of millennial, but I am one nonetheless) and I can attest to that statistic. When I was an employee, I only lasted about two years in each job, and even my best employees stay for only about two years.

Turnover is, unfortunately, part of running a business. People move on for a variety of reasons, and you want your firm to not depend on anyone. As the *E-Myth* says, you want to be systems-dependent instead of people-dependent. That is what this case management system ensures for you.

Every single client communication needs to be recorded in the case management system. Whether it is a call, email, letter, text message, in-person meeting, form review meeting, trial prep, etc, it all has to be recorded in the case management system.

While this is a great way to ensure that everything is well documented in case, if there are any future issues in the case, it has a more important benefit....

If a client calls, anyone should be able to see the latest information because of the case management system. There is *no reason at all that someone should need to ask you about the case*. The notes and messages will record every single action: phone calls, case submission, updates on what is needed from the client, attorney responses to client questions, and more.

All Case Communications Go Through the Case Management System

You are no longer going to email within your team about cases. Ever. Never ever ever. Your inbox is going to thank you. You will actually feel like you can get your inbox under control and get your interruptions under control.

If there's a question about a case:

- Your team will ask you through the case management system, and you will respond through the case management system *only*.

- No emails, e-chats, in-person talking, etc, about the cases. It's all done through the case management system.

Unless there are emergencies, your clients also go through the case management system.

- Your assistant takes calls and will answer any questions they can.

- If the questions are legal questions, then your assistant will note the questions and refer them to you through the case management system.

- You will then respond through the case management system. And the assistant will call the client and say, "The lawyer says [information relayed through the case management system]."

- This is an important way to log what information is given to the client and when.

- It is also a reference point for all people working on a case. They can find out anything they need to know through the case notes and messages.

- As discussed earlier, if the client wants to talk to the lawyer only, then that person will be scheduled for a phone meeting.

This is especially great for those of us who have techy clients. Many case management systems allow for the client to have their own login and portal, which allows clients to communicate with you directly through the system.

If your clients are even a tiny bit tech-savvy, it is a great idea to require this for your clients. Put it in your contract. Tell them that they are not allowed to email you, they can only write to you through their client portal.

If you follow all of these steps, you will officially not be the keeper of information in your law firm any long. And now you can access case-related information from anywhere in the world at any time, meaning you can work and manage your cases from anywhere so long as you have an internet connection.

Organization by Case Process

Maximize your use of the case management system with a quick way to determine the Active, Pending, and Waiting on the Client cases.

At my firm, we decided to indicate this by putting a letter and a dash at the beginning of the client's name.

This coding makes things SO much easier:

Active cases = A-

Pending cases= P-

Waiting on the Client cases= Y-

- When a client calls and wants to know what's going on in her case, if you see the P-, you instantly know that it's pending.

- If it's Y- you can go into the client's case in the system and see what it is that you are waiting on.

- If it's A- you can tell the client that you are working on it.

- We send an update letter to our clients each month telling them that their cases are active, pending, or that we are waiting on them.

  o Our admin also finds it easy to determine which letter to send, simply based on the letter in our system. It makes client communication so efficient and easy.

- This makes it easy to check in on things that need to be done, too.

  o If you run a case report of all of your cases, it will group the As together, the Ps together, and the Ys together, so that you'll be able to see all of the cases in each category. I had one assistant who would run case reports each day to see what was active so she could prioritize it.

Our goal is always to get cases into P. But as I mentioned earlier, when the clients come in to sign, that same day they are either put into Pending or into Waiting on the Client. We either mail out or we have to follow up with the client.

The moment after a case is submitted, the assistant updates the case from A- to P-, and it feels so good!

In our case review meetings, our goal is to always have one page or less of As and under five cases in Y. If we have a lot of As, it usually means that we are opening a lot of new cases, and it can also be a signal that my staff needs more help and support—either from me or contract attorneys.

It's a great way to keep you and your team organized. Once you start using this system, you will never go back.

Do Your Consultations in Your Case Management System

Create a "consult" case right inside your case management system instead of using hand-written notes or Word!

- Take notes directly into the system.

- When the client comes in to sign up, you will be able to reference all of the important information that you noted in the consult.

- It's immediately a part of their case management e-files.

- In most case management systems, you can label the case types.

    o Be sure to label the case type a "consult," and then when they sign up, instead of opening a new e-case in the case management system, just change the case type.

    o This preserves the consultation notes.

- Later, you can check the consultation notes to make sure that nothing is inconsistent with what they first told you, or see if there's an important fact or circumstance that happened to be left out.

- If clients don't sign but come back for consult again, you will be able to review your notes, pick up where you left off, and have a meaningful conversation about next steps and what, if anything, has changed.

Calendaring in Your Case Management System

Pretty much every case management system syncs with your calendars, such as iCal, Google Calendar, and others. You can see everything on your phone's calendar, and keep yourself organized through your personal calendaring system and professional calendaring system.

Many case management systems also have an app with the calendar too which is one more way to keep organized. They have reminders, tasks, ways to assign tasks and reminders, and more!

No more need for a paper calendaring backup when you have a case management system that can provide you access to your calendar across so many different platforms!

Also, it's usually very easy to set up the calendar syncing with the case management system. These companies have great tech support for you.

Handling Email Overwhelm

Email started off as one of the best inventions, but now some days it feels more like a curse than a blessing. Email can be distracting, overwhelming, and all-consuming. Our inboxes are overflowing with client emails, staff emails, listservs, personal emails, mailing lists, and more. I think that most of us have found ourselves, at some point, completely drowning in emails.

There are some quick and easy ways to get your emails under control right away. Some we have already talked about, but they are worth mentioning again:

- Within your firm, there should be no internal emails about cases. All cases are discussed via the case management system.

- Require that your clients communicate with you strictly through the case management system—no emails.

- Set up a firm email account where all communications go. So much of you and your team's day can be consumed by responding to emails. We made a general email address where all emails from clients go. It is monitored by everyone and is responded to only by the admin. This way if someone ever leaves the firm, all of the emails are in one place. We can also make sure that all communications are responded to right away and ensure that the wording and messaging are consistent.

  - It is always a fear that one person on your team can't handle emails well. Then if emails start falling through the cracks, including emails with client docs, you will never know it. But with the main firm email, this will not happen because the account is being monitored constantly.

- Set up an email address for any certain case type that sends a lot of confirmation emails and unimportant emails. For example, we have to email a certain address that always kicks back auto responders and also sends a lot of email communications. Before, it was flooding my inbox with 20-50 emails a day. So we made an email address where all of those communications go. We file things from that email address, and respond through that email address. The person in our office who is in charge of those communications checks and handles that email address. (In our firm, it is criminal records requests and immigration file requests.) It has helped the email overwhelm so much and ensured that we have consistency with our requests and their responses.

- Use labels and archiving.

  - We have labels for all different types of emails. So I stick the label on it, and then I can archive it. That way all of my emails are out of my inbox, but they are also not lost in cyber world. They are neatly tucked away in their inbox folders where I can reference them as needed.

- Use Boomerang

  - Boomerang is something you can add to your email account, at least for Google for Business users, that allows you to schedule email follow ups, send out regular emails, and, best of all, take an email out of your inbox and bring it back on a certain date.

  - Oftentimes I leave an email sitting in my inbox, because I know I will need to respond to it, but I don't have the information that I need yet in order to respond. So I will have it resent on a certain date. Or if it is an email that requires a response a certain number of days later, with boomerang I can get it out of my inbox for now, and I can choose what day it will be brought back into my inbox as a "new" email so I can work on it then.

  - It's a great way to keep my inbox clear AND make sure I don't miss responding to important emails.

- Get a virtual assistant

- It helps tremendously if you can have someone on the back end managing this for you. My virtual assistant creates the labels for my email, puts the labels on the emails, responds to emails as me when appropriate, flags emails for my review and reminds me to respond to emails when I haven't responded on time, drafts emails for me that I dictate to her, archives emails for me, and more.

- There are tons of VA services out there—I found my VA through an expat group. She had never been a VA before, but we have worked it out and learned a lot together! With a VA, it does take some trial and error before you find the right person and get the right set up, but once you get things flowing, it will be the best thing that has ever happened to you!

Now, get working on Inbox Zero! It can be a reality for you!

Schedule Client Communications

You've worked hard to cut down on your interruptions throughout the day. You have a system for dealing with the questions that come from your team. You have a way to communicate about cases that does not interrupt your day or their days. But what about clients?

Clients want to hear from you regularly, and they want to make sure things are going well with their cases. This results in phone calls, emails, and drop-ins. If you don't have a system for handling these client communications, they can drain your time and take you away from the other work that you need to get done.

One of the first things to do is to start communicating with your clients *first*.

Give them so many updates on their cases that they don't need to communicate with you, because you are communicating with them so much. By sending monthly letters and emails to clients about whether their cases are active, pending, or you are waiting on them, it is going to significantly cut down on their need to call you or come by.

As discussed in the previous section, you can use Boomerang.

- Add it to your email.

- Use it to schedule emails to clients on Gmail.

- o Schedule weekly check-in emails to say, "Everything is going well. If you have any questions, don't hesitate to reach out."

- Set it and forget it.

- The clients feel very nurtured and assured that their cases are important. All with the click of a button!

It's an interesting phenomenon that when you reach out to the client, it is almost always a positive experience from both sides.

- Clients are happy to hear from you. They are glad to know that you are working on their cases and that you care about their cases.

- You get to control the conversation—meaning that you decide when to call.

  - o You are prepared for the call. You have reviewed your notes, and you know what you want to say. Even if it's just, "Hi there, just wanted to give you a call to let you know that everything is going well in your case."

- If the client beats you to a call and insists on talking to you, have your assistant schedule the client for a 15-minute phone meeting.

  - o This makes the call formal and professional instead of emotional.

  - o You can review the case and be refreshed with what is going on.

  - o The client will also have thought through any questions or concerns and be able to articulate himself best.

Make use of the one-hour slot I mentioned in the Client Phone Calls module in "Chapter 7: Client Experience." Do that and reserve an hour to take these kinds of calls. This way, it doesn't disrupt your day.

Clients love this. It's a meeting. It's scheduled. And because you are so well-prepared in that phone call, they feel really cared for, and they feel like they are very important to you.

It maximizes time, increases client satisfaction, and still allows you to make more money by not giving up precious money-making slots in your day. It's a win-win-win!

Workbook

Now it's your turn! Go to page 20 of the Workbook and fill out the exercises for Chapter 1. Visit: http://bit.ly/LFBS-Book

Afterward

This book should have given you some ways to take immediate action in your cases right now. Do not allow yourself to get overwhelmed. Pick one area to tackle right now. Yes, I mean **right now**! Don't delay. Your success is in your hands. It's exciting! Take the steps forward today to have a firm and life that is better than you have ever dreamed.

Perhaps you need to identify your personal stories and shift your mindset on money, perfectionism, and your practice? It starts there. You need to align everything in your mind before you can move forward and achieve the successful firm in your vision.

When it comes to vision and strategy, it really helps to write things down. If you haven't yet, go back to "Chapter 2: Vision and Strategy" and answer the questions. Lay down your plans and ambitions so you can start working toward making them reality.

And remember, your firm can make your dreams a reality. You just need to be creative and assertive. Earn what you are worth!

Your firm can only stand if you have a foundation of good finances. You need money to do the work you love and continue serving your clients. Doing great work and earning a great living are not mutually exclusive propositions. You can and should do both.

You bring value. Big value. All those years in school and years of experience translate to a very unique expertise that only you can bring your client. Make sure your office, websites, print materials, consultations, and staff communicate this unique advantage.

Let your unique brand unite you and your firm. With the help of training and policy manuals, your staff will be able to operate under your brand and your firm's values.

Your brand and values should be firmly established. That's how you discover and connect with your Ideal Clients. You save time and money in marketing, because you focus your campaigns to attract your Ideal Client—and you succeed!

Once you have your Ideal Clients, it's a matter of making sure their experience with your firm turns them into your voluntary marketing army. Client experience and customer service are integral to any business—and that includes your firm. Your service is not just legal work.

Finally, with juggling all the above, you need efficiency. It shouldn't have to be juggling at all! It should be more like a well-oiled machine running smoothly. You need to implement systems and make your firm as independent as it's able to be.

Altogether, these can and will launch your firm to success, without you working yourself to the bone every day, every week.

Now get out there and get started!

If you need support in any way, please feel free to email directly at **ally@allylozano.com**. I would love to help guide you along the way. And if you want monthly business support, please join my Six Figure Solo membership. I go deep into different business topics each month and a coaching and consulting call.

I wish you tons of success as you build your law firm into a thriving business. Be consistent. Keep showing up and doing the work. I promise you it will pay off.

To Six Figures and Beyond,

Ally

Law Firm Business School Course

Do you want to take the lessons from this book to the next level?

Join the Law Firm Business School course!

The 8-week long course will help hold you accountable to all you have learned. Each week you will have access to modules on-demand with workbooks to help you apply your new tools to your practice.

Additionally, there is a private Facebook group just for the Law Firm Business Schoolers where you can share what you have learned, ask questions, and more.

As a part of the online course, you will also get the bonus of the Ally Lozano Sales Academy which will super-charge your sales and uplevel your revenues.

To learn more go to **www.LawFirmBusinessSchool.com**

Six Figure Solo

Need more support as you are taking your business to next level? Join Six Figure Solo! Each and every month I bring you business tools and strategies that are instantly applicable to helping you have more success in your law firm. With a monthly Power Hour webinar, Ask Ally Q&A coaching session, private Facebook group, discounts on courses and conferences, and more, you can't afford to miss it!

With membership at only $30/month, you get top-notch business tools for cheaper than a week's worth of your favorite latte!

To learn more go to **www.AllyLozano.com/SixFigure**

Other books by author

Be the CEO of Your Law Firm: Gain Control, Turn a Profit, and Reclaim Your Life

Ignite Your Practice with the T Visa: A Guide for Immigration Lawyers

About the author

Alexandra "Ally" Lozano is a best-selling author and award-winning attorney. She is the founder of Alexandra Lozano Immigration Law PLLC, with offices in Seattle and Los Angeles. In 2015, her law firm went from struggling to make ends meet to earning six figures in less than three months, and by 2017 she earned into the seven figures. Ally is passionate about teaching other attorneys how they can transform a law practice into a thriving business. She empowers attorneys to be the CEOs of their law firms with her weekly blog, webinars, inspirational 6Minute CEO Podcast, Six Figure Solo Membership, and the annual Women, Power & Money in-person conference where she provides women attorneys with step-by-step guidance on how to do the work they love while running a profitable legal business. She is also the founder of the international network, Amiga Lawyers, the Association of Mother Immigration Attorneys (AMIGA). Her personal website is www.allylozano.com. She lives in the Seattle area with her husband and their five children.

CPSIA information can be obtained
at www.ICGtesting.com
Printed in the USA
LVHW040227030520
654902LV00003B/690